Tony & Chris Grogan

# A Dales High Way

## Route Guide

2020
Published by Skyware Ltd.

# INTRODUCTION

In September 2007 we set off to walk from our home in Saltaire to Appleby-in-Westmorland.

Following ancient trade routes, green lanes and packhorse trails wherever possible, we walked north. Each day brought new excitement as we explored the spectacular landscapes of the high country, until finally, in the lush Eden Valley, the Norman tower of Appleby Castle came into view.

The walking was over but there was still much enjoyment to come as we returned to Saltaire on England's most beautiful railway, the Settle - Carlisle line, glimpsing along the way the glories of the previous eight days.

A Dales High Way was born.

The 90 mile route covers some of the most beautiful scenery in the Yorkshire Dales from the darkly mysterious Rombalds Moor, with its Stone Age rock art, to the dramatic limestone scars of Malhamdale.

It meanders along the banks of the River Ribble, where in autumn salmon can be seen leaping up the waterfalls of Stainforth Force, and passes the isolated splendour of Sunbiggin Tarn. It climbs mighty Ingleborough, favourite of the Yorkshire Three Peaks, and in a breathtaking six-mile ridge walk crosses the velvety folds of the Howgill Fells.

The route divides naturally into 6 sections: Rombalds Moor, Malhamdale, Ingleborough, Dentdale, the Howgill Fells and the Eden Valley.

Seasoned walkers might tackle one section a day, but most people will find the first 2 sections too long. It is better to break them and take time to explore. The walk can be conveniently undertaken in 8 days, say Saturday to Saturday, with plenty of time then to enjoy the market towns and villages on the way.

*Below:* The Ribble above Settle.   *Opposite:* Trench Woods, Saltaire.

| Day 1: | Saltaire to Ilkley | 7.5 miles |
| --- | --- | --- |
| Day 2: | Ilkley to Skipton | 11.4 miles |
| Day 3: | Skipton to Malham | 12.9 miles |
| Day 4: | Malham to Stainforth | 10.3 miles |
| Day 5: | Stainforth to Chapel-le-Dale | 11.6 miles |
| Day 6: | Chapel-le-Dale to Sedbergh | 15.7 miles |
| Day 7: | Sedbergh to Newbiggin-on-Lune | 10.9 miles |
| Day 8: | Newbiggin-on-Lune to Appleby | 12.7 miles |

The total of 93 miles above includes diversions into Ilkley, Malham and Stainforth.

Accommodation is generally plentiful except at Chapel-le-Dale so book there first or head for Ribblehead. Staying at Ribblehead (pub or bunkbarn) adds an extra 1.9 miles on day 5 but saves 2.7 miles the following day. For details please check the Dales High Way website www.daleshighway.org.uk

The high terrain covered by the walk is exposed and it can be very cold and wet on the fell tops, even in summer. Bad weather and thick mist can descend quickly, so be prepared. The guide includes alternative bad weather routes for the highest sections, Ingleborough and the Howgill Fells.

The maps cover only the immediate route in detail, so the appropriate OS map and a compass are essential. Most of the route is covered by 2 maps: OL2 and OL19. Unfortunately parts of Section 1 are covered by 2 others; the most useful is Explorer 297, with the first 2 miles covered by Explorer 288.

Watch out also for the distinctive Dales High Way waymarks.

The route sticks mostly to established rights of way but in a few places follows well-used tracks across open access land. Occasionally, in case of fire risk for example, restrictions may be imposed on these parts. Please follow suggested or obvious diversions.

*Above:* Victoria Hall, Saltaire.   *Below:* Appleby Horse Fair.

*Below:* Crossing Rombalds Moor towards Ilkley.

# SALTAIRE

The model village of Saltaire was built by the Victorian wool baron Sir Titus Salt. Following the completion of Salts Mill in 1853 he built houses for his workers, as well as shops, wash and bath-houses, a hospital, school, almshouses, allotments, a park and an institute, all of which can be seen today.

Salt had moved production from his textile mills in Bradford to a greenfield site on the banks of the River Aire, adjoining the railway and canal. It got his workers away from Bradford where the appalling conditions were the cause of growing unrest. In 1846 George Weerth had written, "If anyone wants to know how a poor sinner is tormented in Purgatory, let him travel to Bradford."

Saltaire became a popular weekend escape for mill workers from Bradford, who enjoyed the canal side, the park and Shipley Glen. The village is still remarkably complete and in 2001 was designated a World Heritage Site by UNESCO.

# APPLEBY-IN-WESTMORLAND

The historic town of Appleby in the lush Eden Valley was originally the county town of Westmorland and has been inhabited for over 1,000 years. The town is dominated by Appleby Castle, a $12^{th}$ century mote and bailey structure which was restored by Lady Anne Clifford in the $17^{th}$ century. Her tomb lies in St Lawrence's Church at the bottom of the wide main street, Boroughgate.

The normally quiet market town erupts every June when thousands of gypsies, travellers and visitors come for the annual Horse Fair. It is one of the largest gypsy gatherings in Europe. Originally cattle and sheep were traded as well as the horses that are the main attraction today. Every day during the fair, horses are brought down from Fair Hill to be washed in the River Eden ready for sale.

# SETTLE - CARLISLE RAILWAY

The Settle-Carlisle railway was the last of the great Victorian construction projects. Work began in 1869 and lasted for 7 years, with 6,000 men working on the line at its peak.

The line crossed bleak, inhospitable, wild country. Shanty towns, with colourful names such as Inkerman, Sebastopol and Jericho, were built along the route to house the navvies and their families. 2,000 people lived in the biggest camp at Batty Green, near Ribblehead. Deaths from accidents and disease were frequent. Over 200 men, women and children are buried at St. Leonard's Church, Chapel-le-Dale alone.

The line was threatened with closure in 1983, but saved after a huge popular campaign. It remains the most spectacular railway journey in England.

*Start your walk with Determination; finish your walk at Peace.*

# 1. ROMBALDS MOOR

## *Saltaire to Skipton   (17.9 miles)*

It is not long into the walk across to Ilkley Moor before the strains and worries of the world begin to lift and the quiet solitude of the wild open moorland takes hold. There is a touch of magic to this ancient landscape, as can be found in the mysterious rock carvings left by prehistoric settlers.

Rombalds Moor rises gently from the south to form a high, heather-clad ridge, lying between Airedale and Wharfedale. It marks the northern end of the Southern Pennine range and is divided into several local moors, including Baildon, Bingley and most famously Ilkley Moor. The land is capped by millstone grit, peat covered, but the going underfoot is suprisingly good, with only a couple of wet patches to cross. The moor is compact and so walkers are never too far from safety, though care is needed in bad weather as distinctive features are few on the bleak uplands.

It was not until the last great ice sheet receded some 14,000 years ago, that the first nomadic people to set foot in the region began to move onto the moor. Thin flint arrowhead slivers of the Middle Stone Age hunter-gatherers (Mesolithic: 9000 - 4000 BC) have been found. More significant are the many enigmatic "cup and ring" rock carvings of their New Stone Age descendants (Neolithic: 4000 - 2000 BC). They began to clear the moors of forest, to settle and farm. Over 400 examples of their rock art have been catalogued across the moor, with as many again on surrounding moors. Their meaning remains a mystery.

Just before the highest point is reached at Lanshaw Lad, you pass the stone circle known as the Twelve Apostles. It is believed to date from the Bronze Age (2000 - 500 BC).

From the Victorian bath house at White Wells, the way follows a truly ancient track along the northern flank of the moor. This forms an impressive long craggy escarpment which dominates the spa town of Ilkley and the Wharfe valley below.

The Swastika Stone, unmissable with its fence, has greeted travellers passing this way since the Iron Age. Watch out for the Neolithic Piper Crag Stone which lies further on. It juts out above the moor edge, 30 metres beyond a gate and down to the right. It is marked with 32 cups with rings and grooves.

From Addingham High Moor the route drops to join the "Roman Road" above Addingham before climbing to Skipton Moor with its impressive vista. Skipton - "the Gateway to the Dales" - is a busy market town, lying in the strategic Aire Gap. The 14th century castle was besieged for 3 years during the English Civil War before the Royalists surrendered. It was partially demolished, but soon restored by the remarkable Lady Anne Clifford. It remains one of the best preserved mediaeval castles in the land and is well worth a visit.

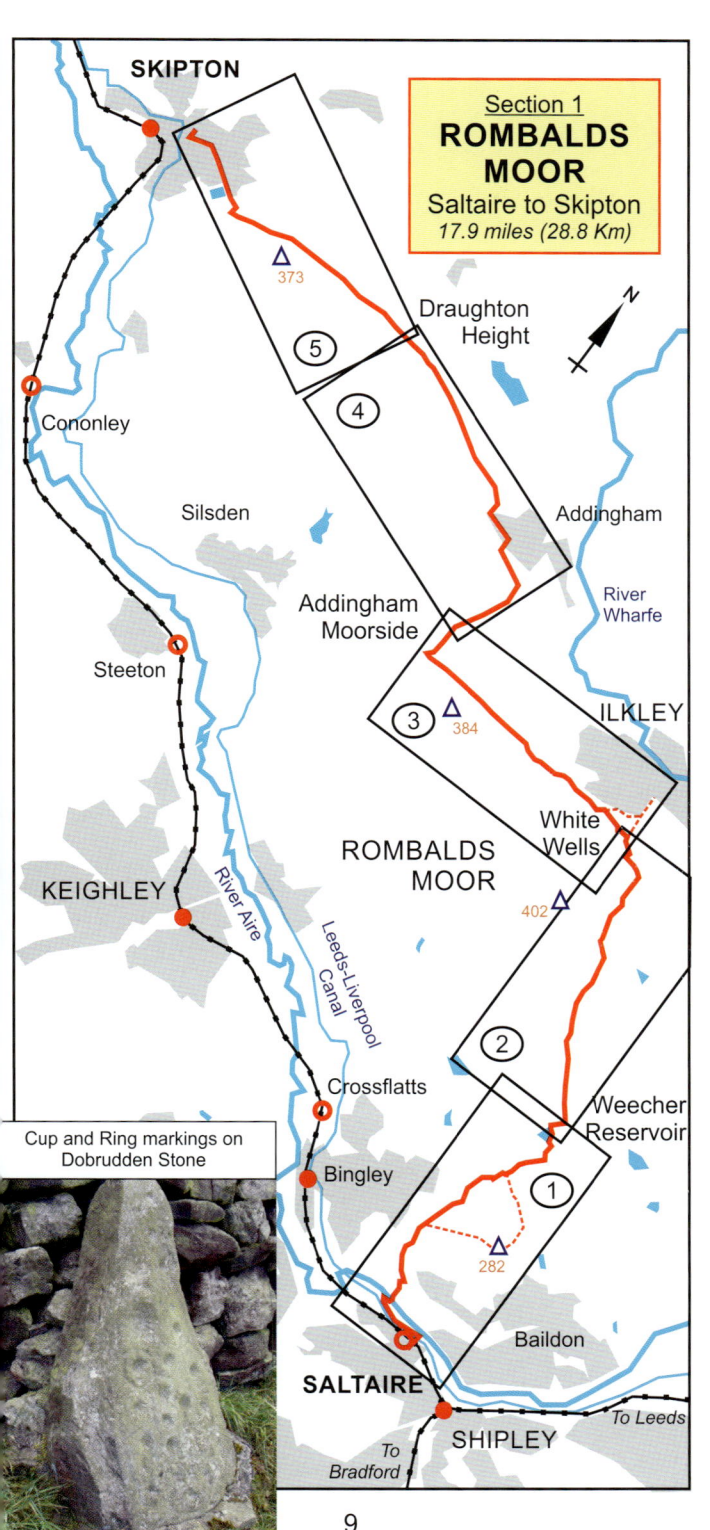

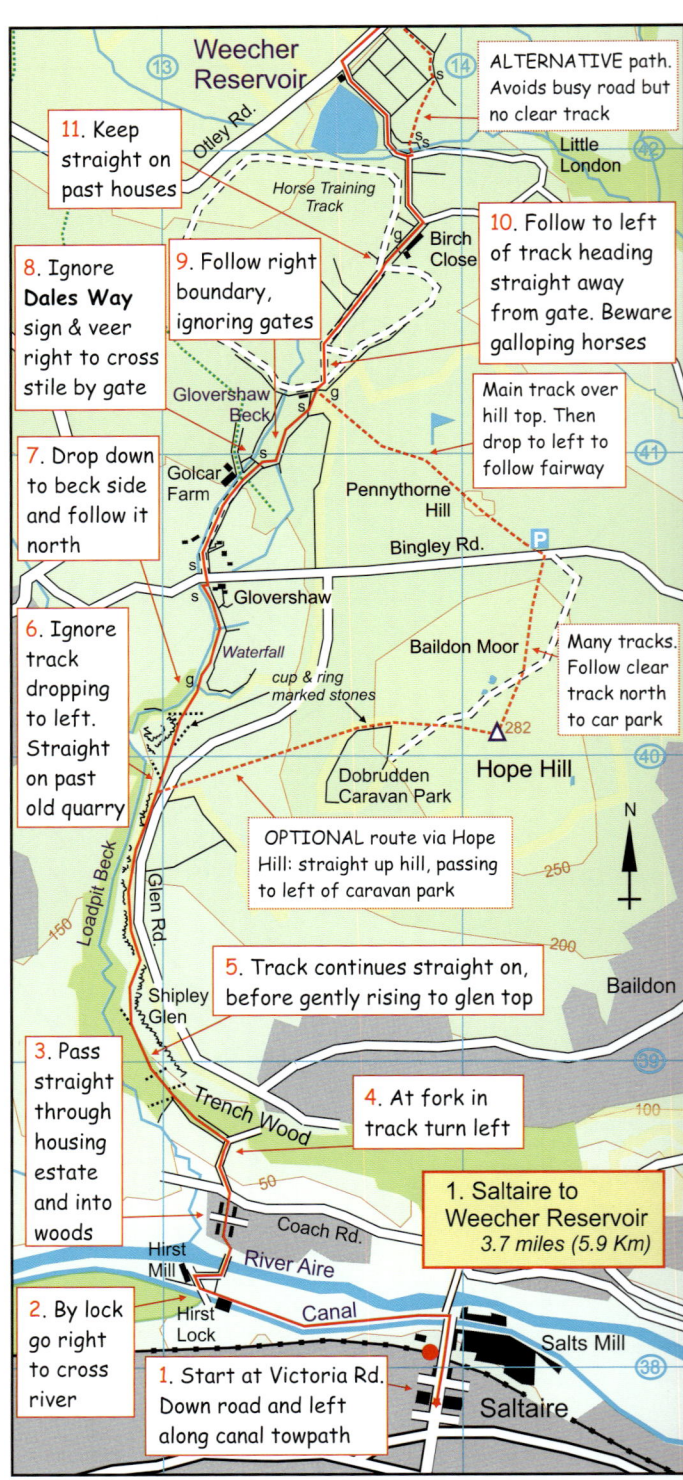

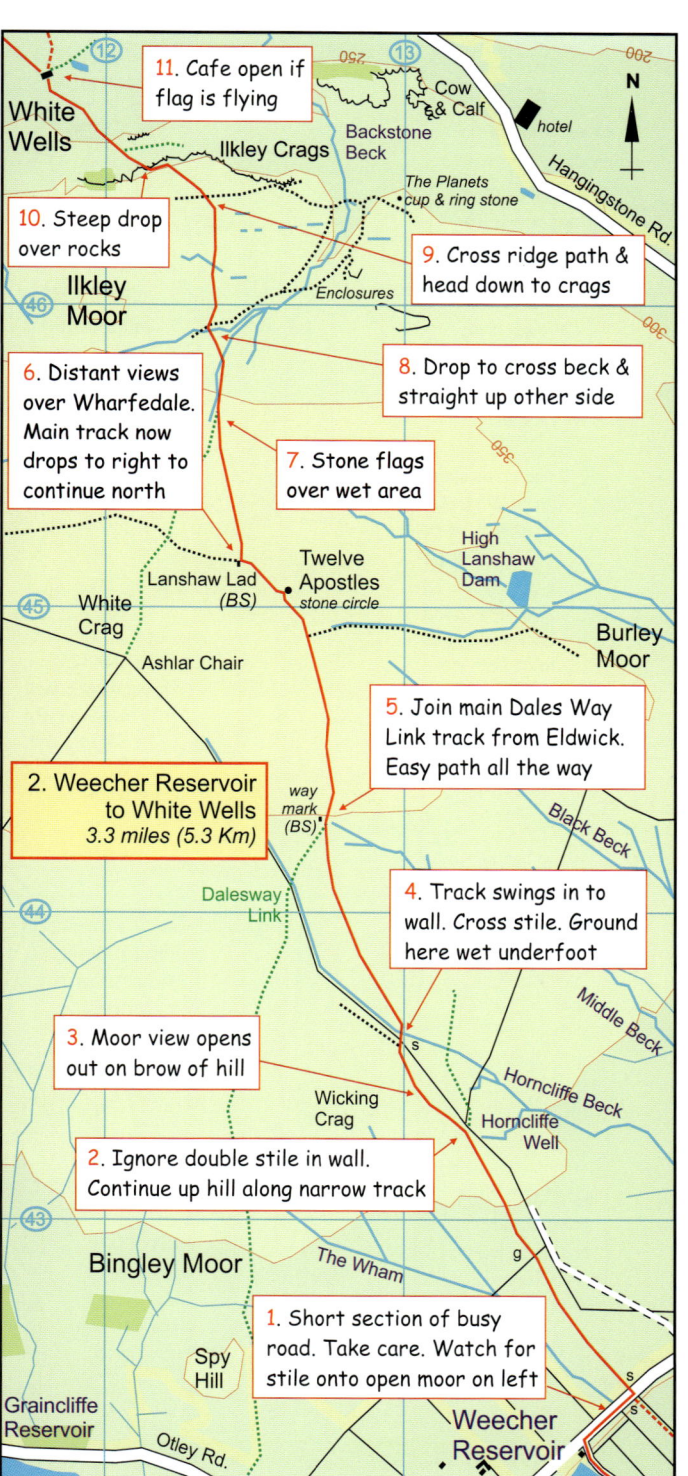

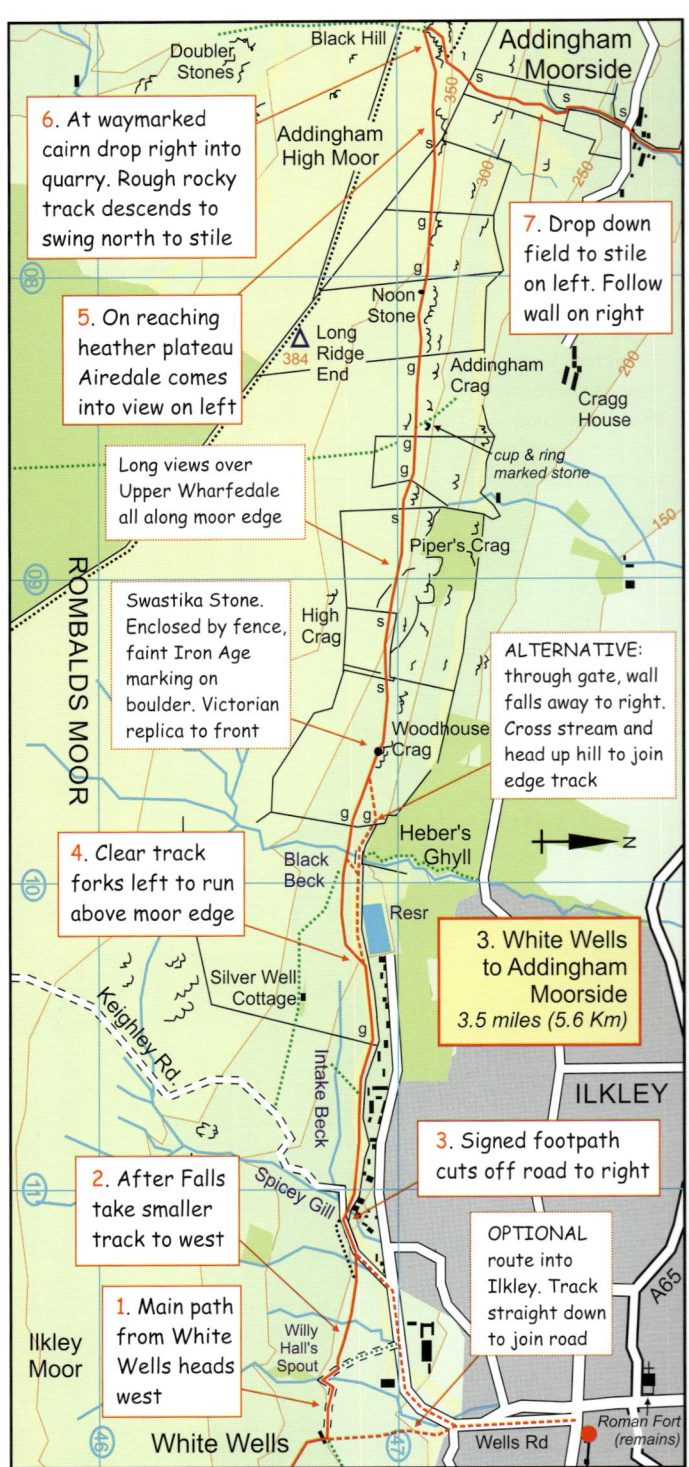

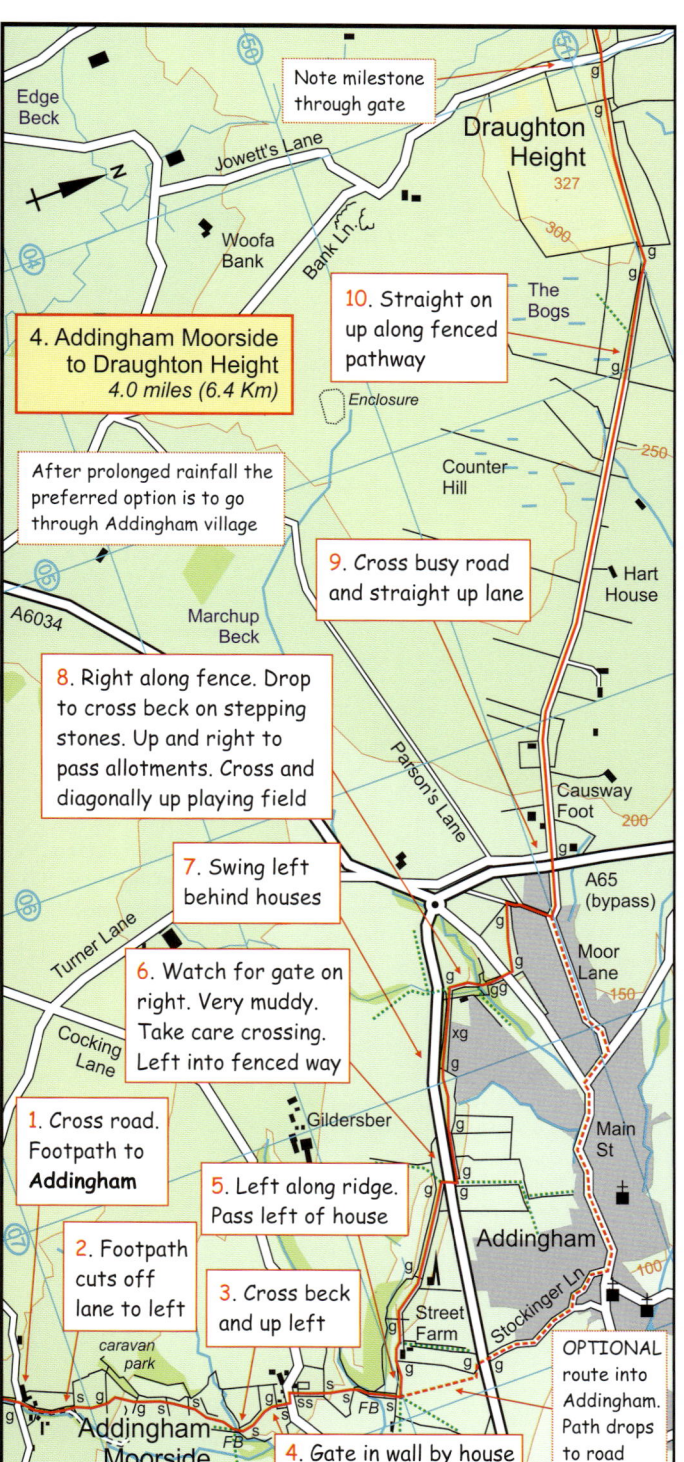

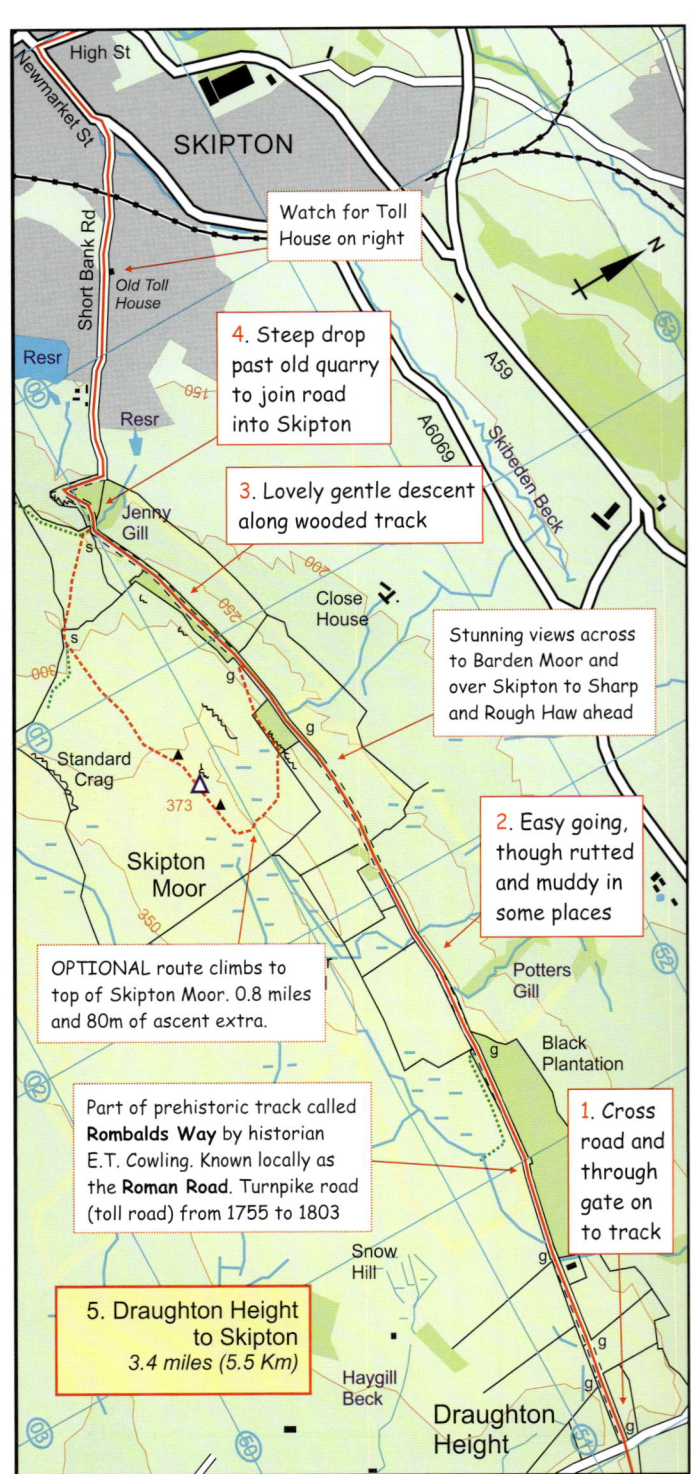

*Above:* Winterburn Reservoir.   *Below:* Gordale Scar

*Below:* Warrendale Knotts and Attermire Scar

## 2. MALHAMDALE

### Skipton to Settle   (18.7 miles)

This section is a tale of two halves, marked by a dramatic and spectacular change in the landscape at Malhamdale.

The climb up Sharp Haw and later to Weets Top covers more of the grassy terrain of Section 1, with a delightful beckside ramble in between to Hetton. This area was immortalised in the film *Calendar Girls* which told the story of Rylstone District Women's Institute and their famous nude calendar.

The panoramic view from Weets Top is magnificent. Here the geological story of the Dales is laid out before you. The rocks of the area are all sedimentary, deposited in water when the region was covered by a shallow tropical sea 350 million years ago. Hundreds of metres beneath your feet is a layer of limestone formed from the calcified remains of tiny marine animals. Above this are layers of shales topped by a hard, impervious layer of millstone grit to give the typical South Pennines moorland you've crossed so far.

Earthquakes produced a long fracture in the rock, the Mid-Craven Fault, which runs across the landscape from east to west. The land north of the fault was pushed upwards, bringing the limestone shelf with it. Later, through the Ice Ages, enormous glaciers scoured away the top layers, carving out the deep, wide dales and leaving islands which became the Three Peaks. As the ice melted, the limestone pavements and scars were exposed in all their glory.

Malham Cove has been cut back from the fault edge by glacial melt waters that once poured down the Dry Valley and cascaded over the Cove in a tremendous waterfall. Goredale Scar is another deep gorge cut by water. A stopover in Malham itself is highly recommended to give time to explore the area. Drop to the village via the waterfall at Janet's Foss.

After climbing up between Kirkby Fell and Grizedales the route passes the impressive Attermire Scar. The first Mesolithic inhabitants sought sanctuary here in caves some 8,000 years or so ago, leaving microflint artefacts as evidence. Victoria Cave, named because it was rediscovered on the day of Queen Victoria's accession in 1837, also contained remains of lion, elephant, rhinoceros, giant deer and hippopotamus dating from the last interglacial period.

Settle is a lovely Dales market town of Anglian origin. It received its Market Charter in 1249 and is at its liveliest on Tuesdays when the weekly market takes place. Settle retains much of its old character with fine Georgian buildings and the unusual 2 storey arched Shambles. The oldest surviving building in the town is the Folly which was built in 1679 and houses the Museum of North Craven Life. At Settle station the Friends of the Settle-Carlisle Line have restored the signal box which is now open to visitors.

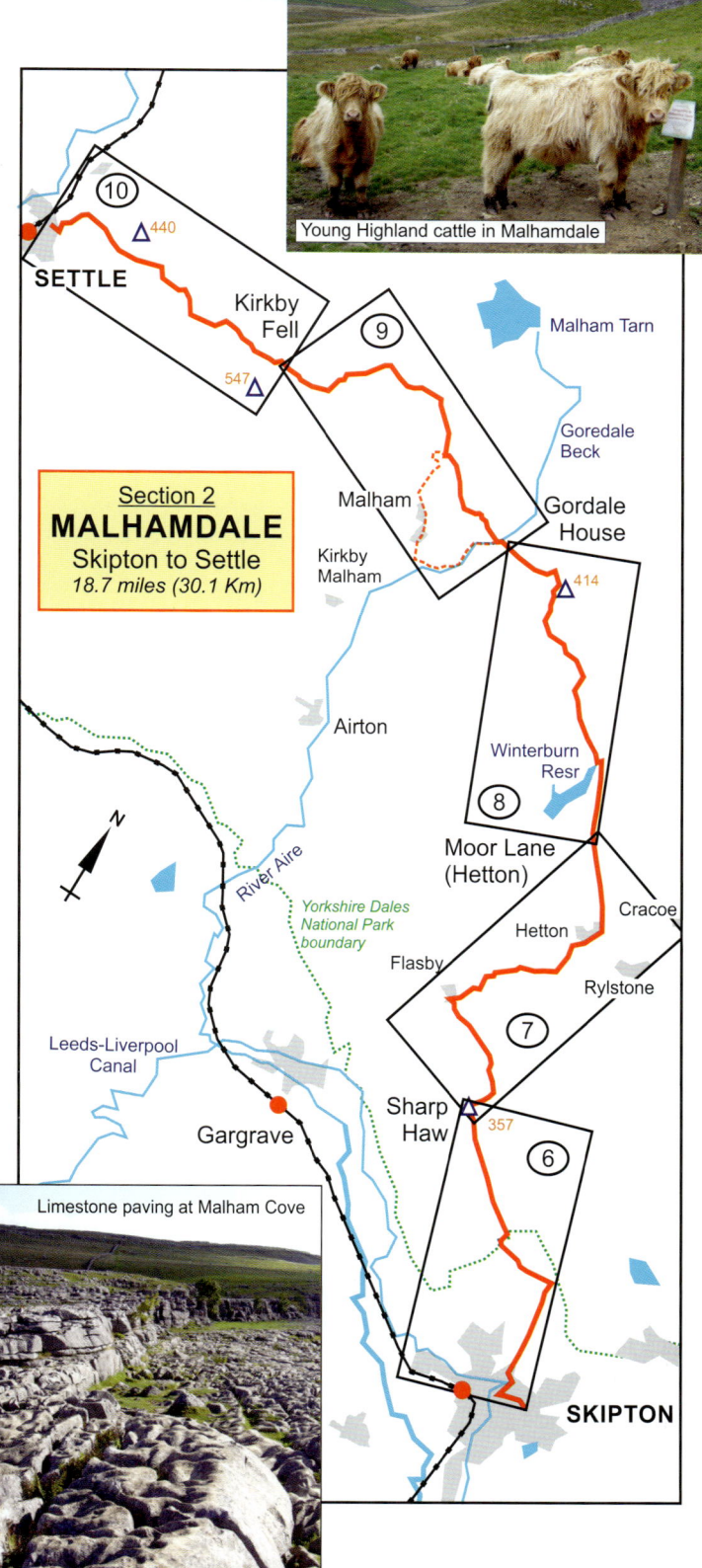

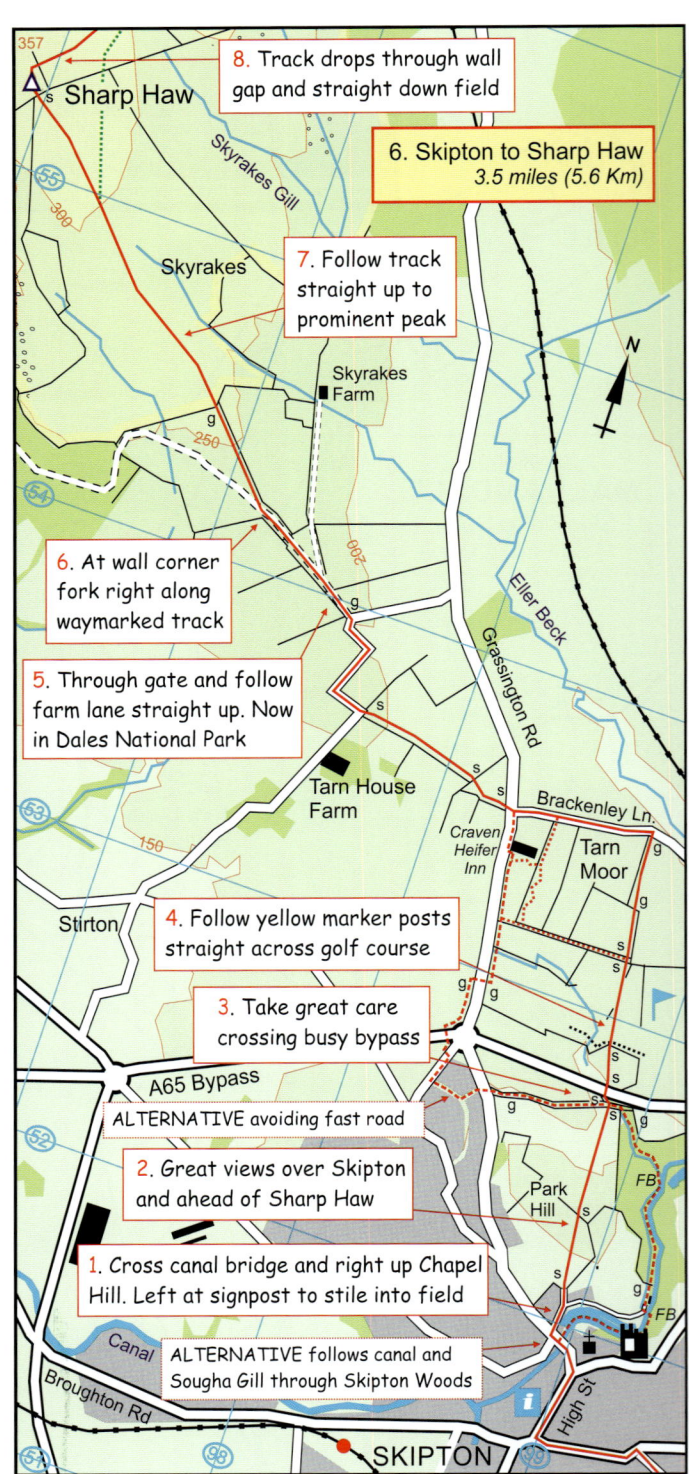

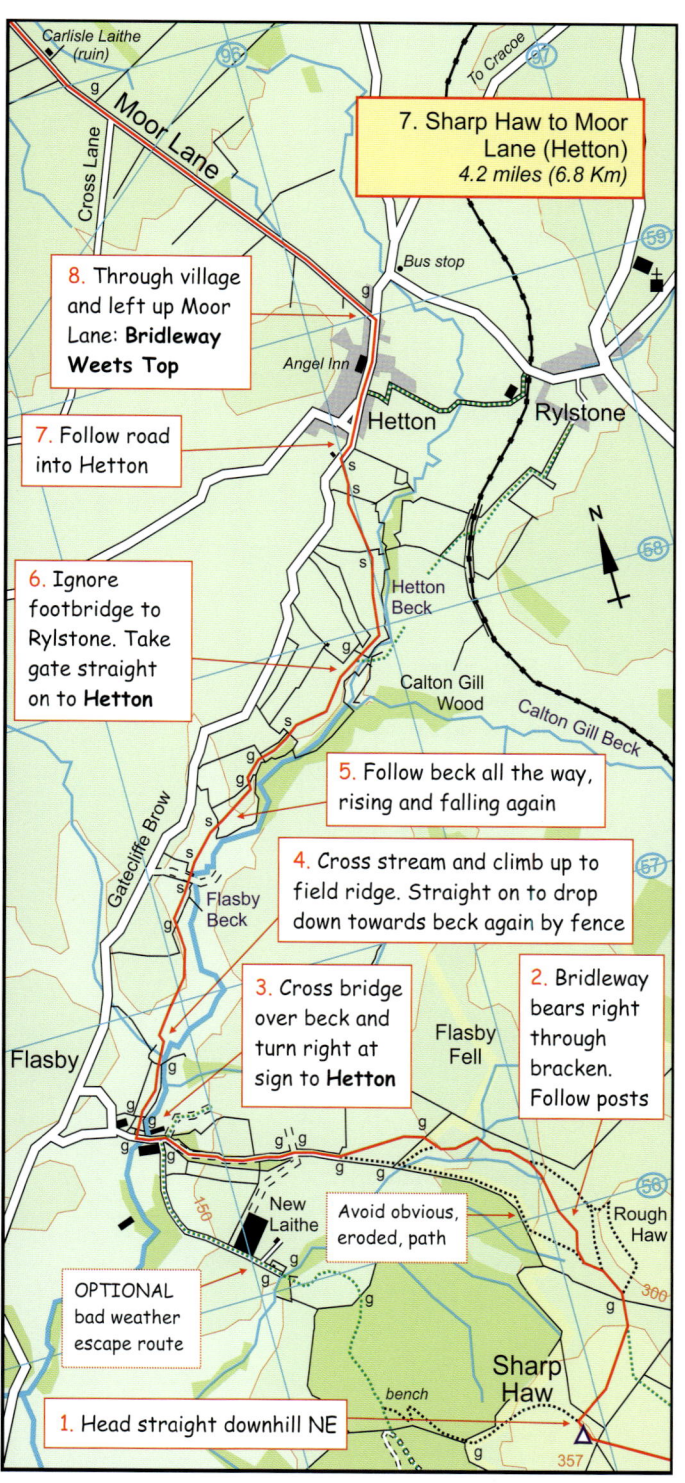

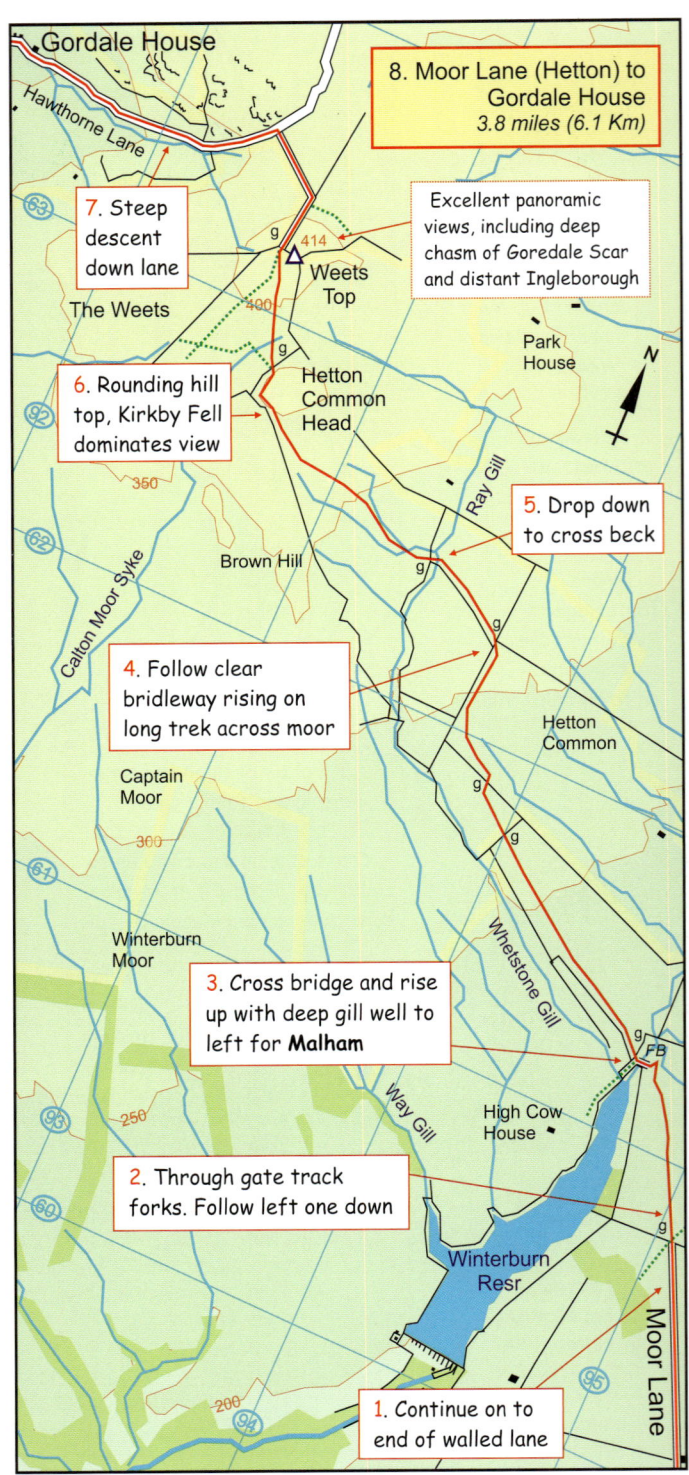

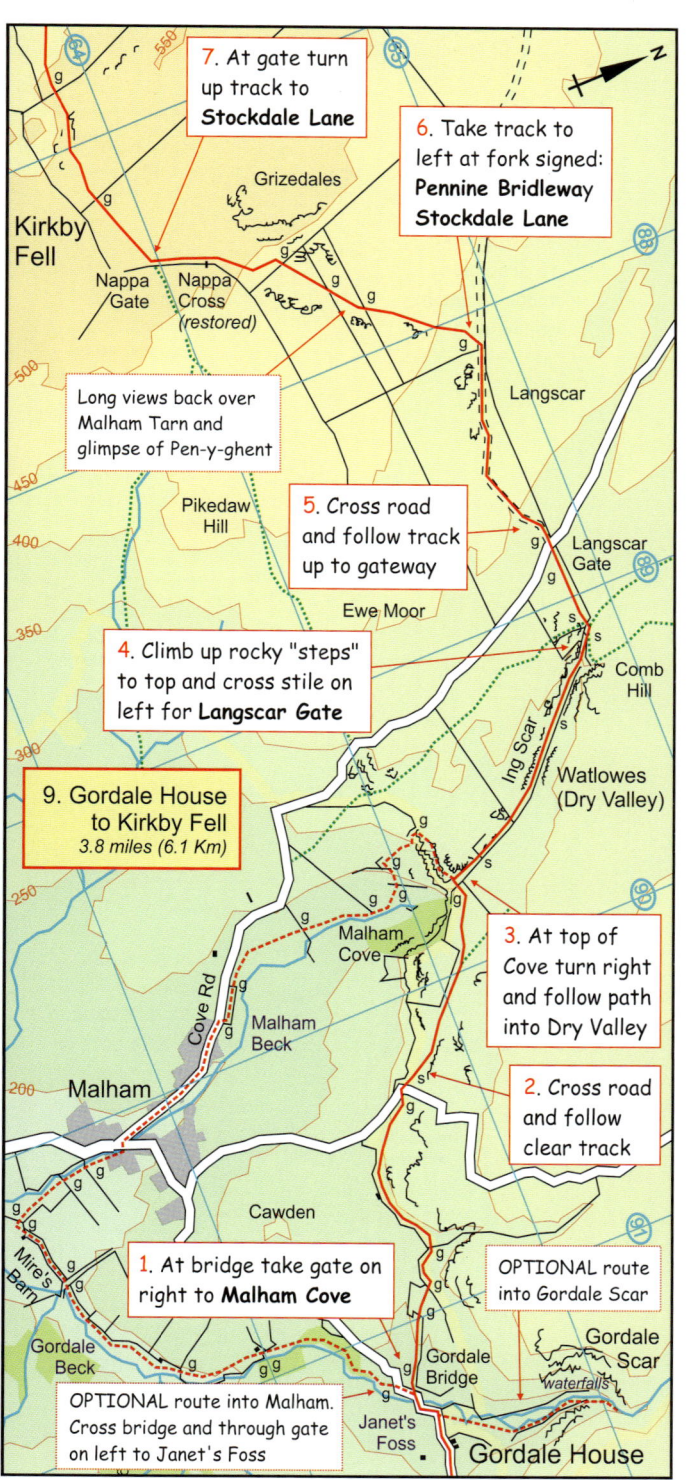

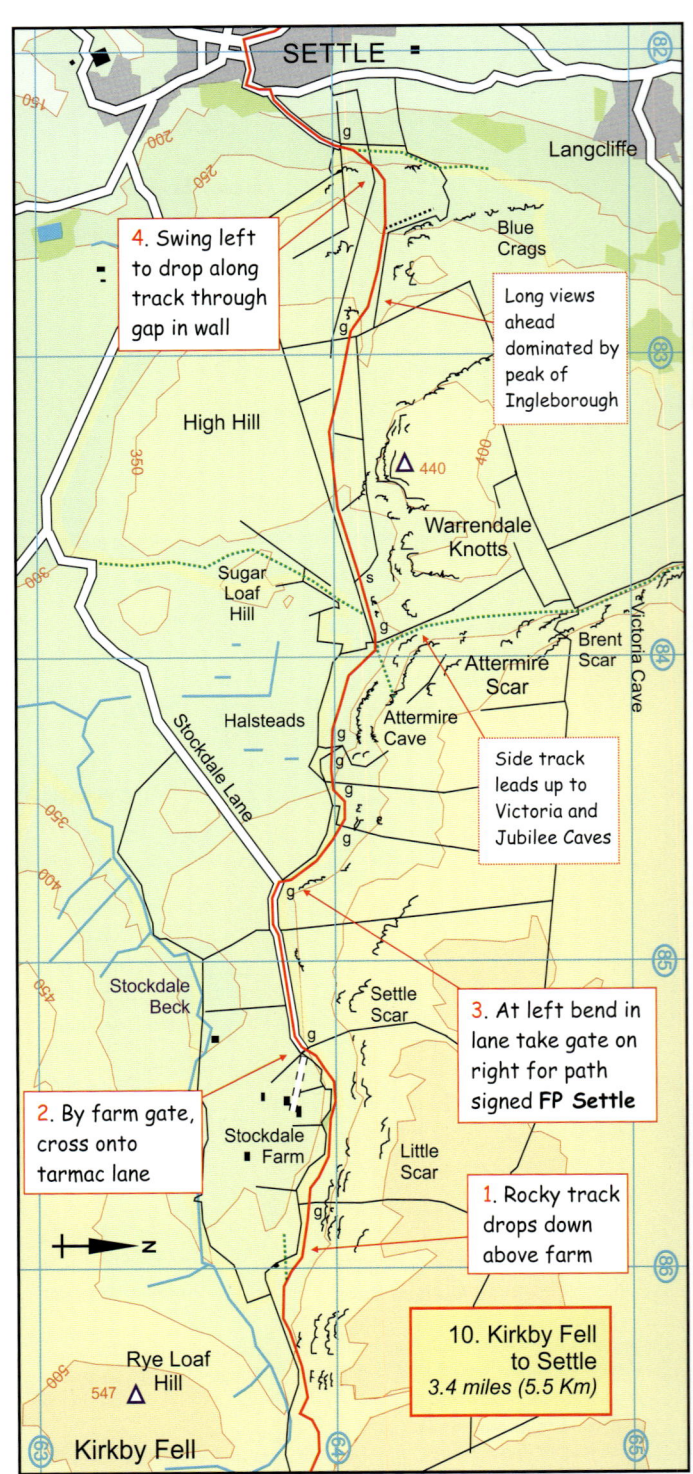

*Above:* Feizor.   *Below:* Clapper Bridge, Crummackdale

*Below:* Limestone plateau at Crummackdale Head

# 3. INGLEBOROUGH

## *Settle to Chapel-le-Dale (14.2 miles)*

The mighty Ingleborough, with its iconic shape, defines this section. The route leads over the top of the mountain before dropping into the quiet and secluded Chapel-le-Dale. This section also offers two alternative routes, should there be problems with accommodation or bad weather.

Capped with hard millstone grit above layers of Yordale shales, Ingleborough sits on a limestone base. The action of acidic water eating into the limestone has created a network of underground holes, tunnels and caverns. This is potholing country, dangerous and deadly to the uninitiated, so don't let curiosity get the better of you. Ingleborough is sometimes called the Hollow Mountain.

From Settle a fine riverside walk along the banks of the Ribble leads to the 14$^{th}$ century packhorse bridge at Little Stainforth. Below is a series of small waterfalls where in autumn you can watch salmon leaping as they struggle upstream to spawn.

From Stainforth the way climbs onto the limestone plateau to pass Smearset Scar before dropping into the southern end of Crummackdale, a lovely and secluded valley.

By Crummack Farm the way climbs again into a dramatic landscape of broad limestone terraces. Some care is needed here, for there are many tracks across this open ground. Follow the major, broad green track as it rises to join Long Lane - the old drove road from Clapham - at the brow.

If the weather is too bad to tackle Ingleborough, continue along this main path via Sulber Gate to Selside, then on to Ribblehead or around the foot of Park Fell to Chapel-le-Dale.

With good weather, a left turn 200 metres on takes a broad track climbing through striking limestone pavements for Ingleborough. If it seems that you are passing the mountain by on your left, don't worry; you are in fact preparing for an ascent via the southern flank of Simon Fell. This is an easy, if lengthy climb.

The rocky summit is vast and offers excellent views all around. On top of the central shelter can be found a metal disk marking all the peaks in view. Amid the rubble you can still discern prehistoric circular features, possibly hut circles, for this may once have been a fortified sanctuary for the Celtic Brigante tribes during the Iron Age and into the period of the Roman Occupation.

Leave the summit the same way you came up, forking left for the startlingly steep but brief descent to Humphrey Bottom and on to the Hill Inn. Those heading for alternative accommodation at Ribblehead can instead follow the ridge edge above the dale, over Open Access Land, for a splendid high level walk across Simon and Park Fells.

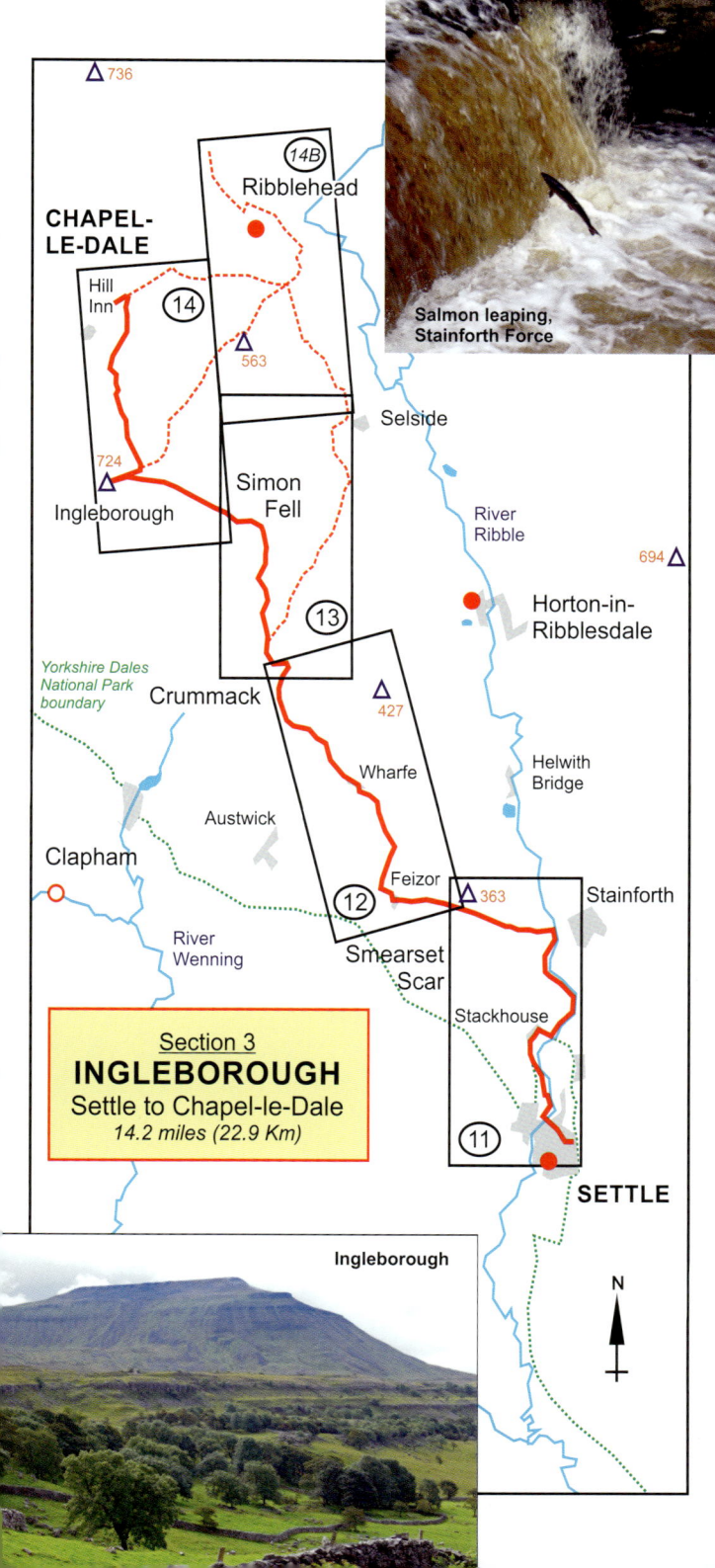

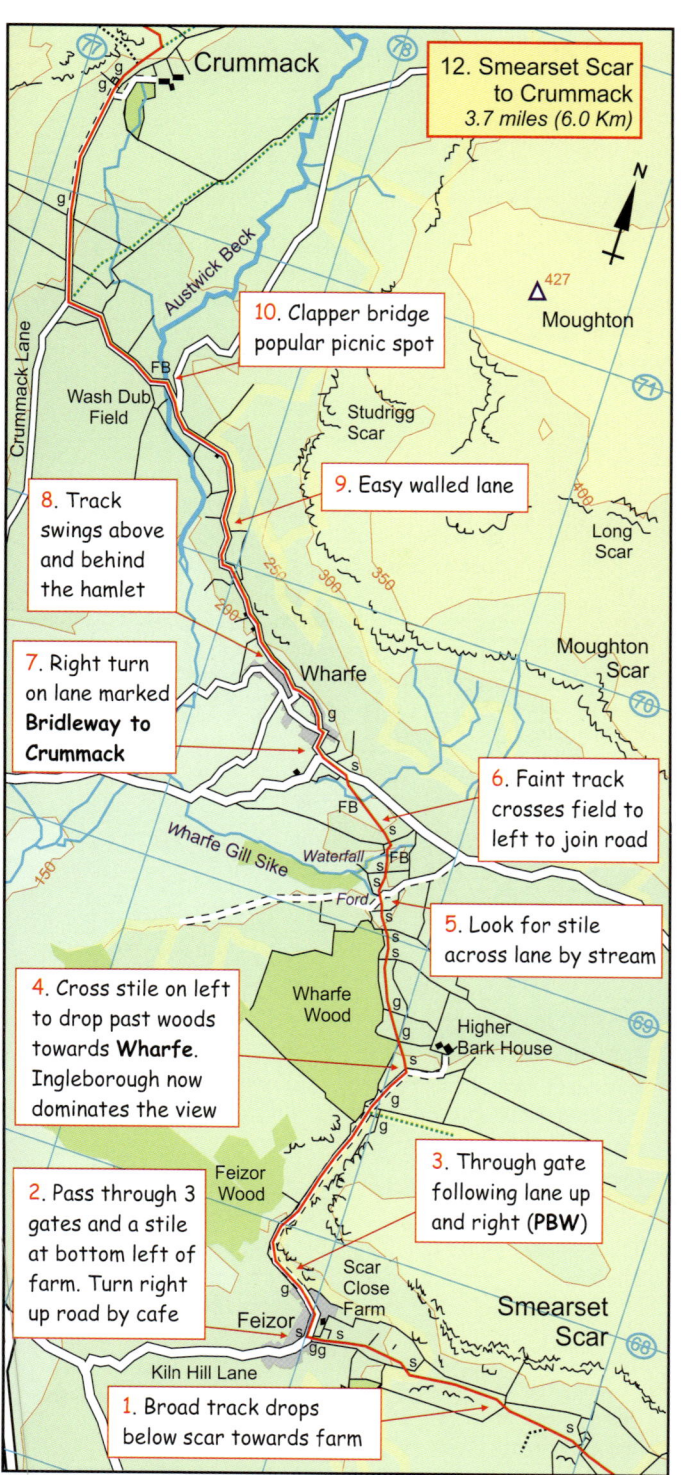

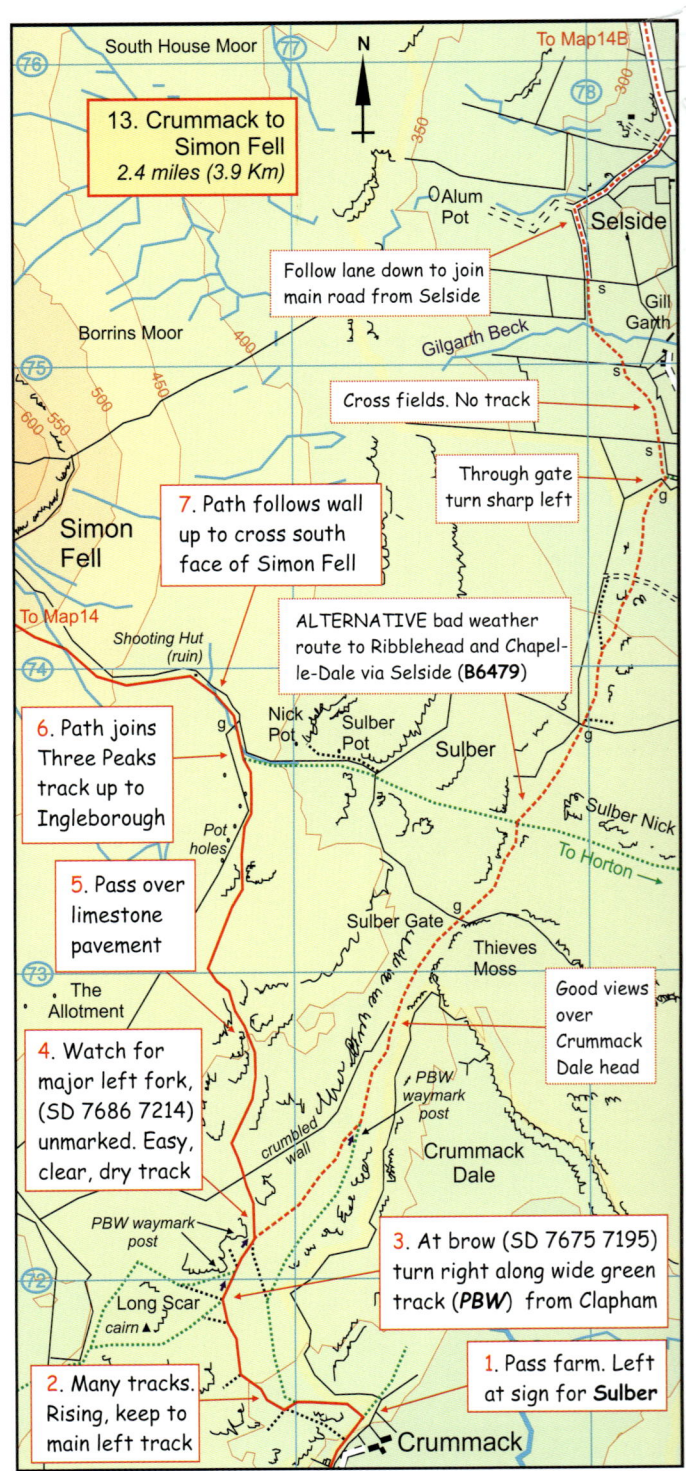

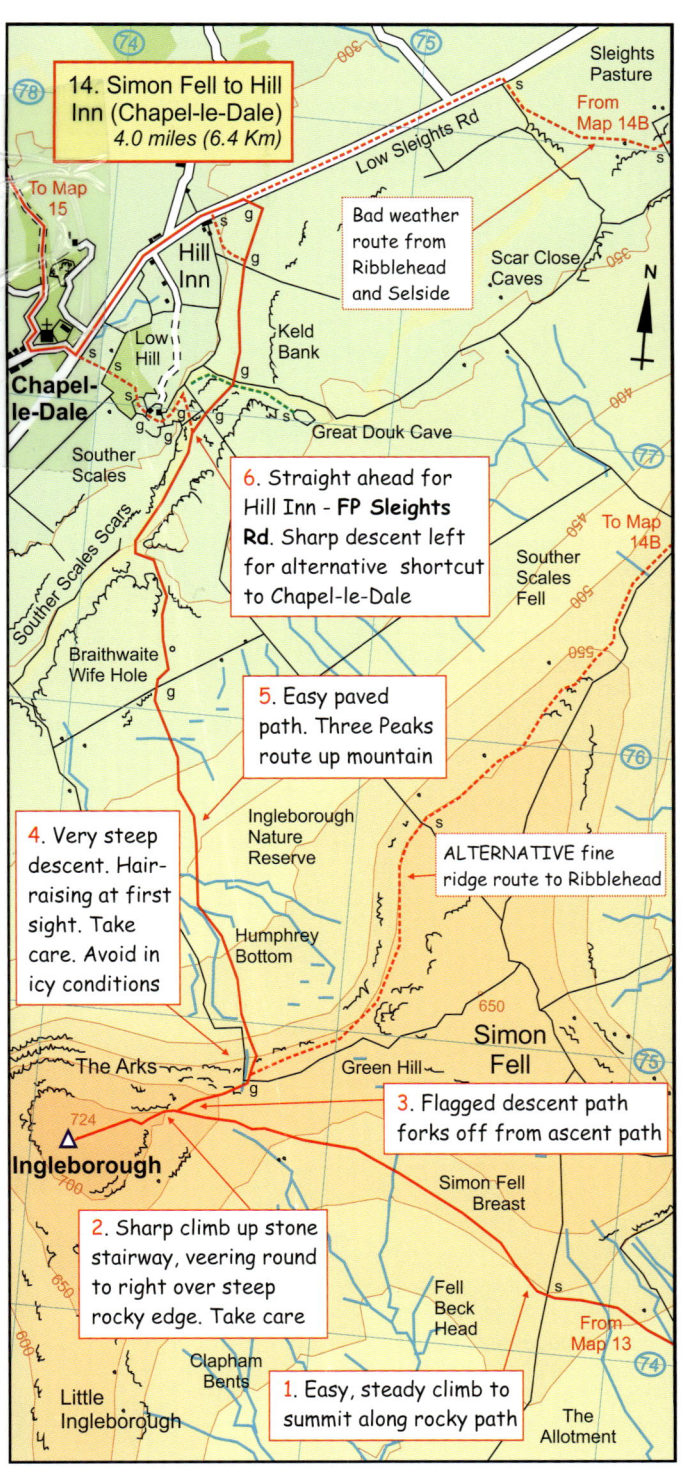

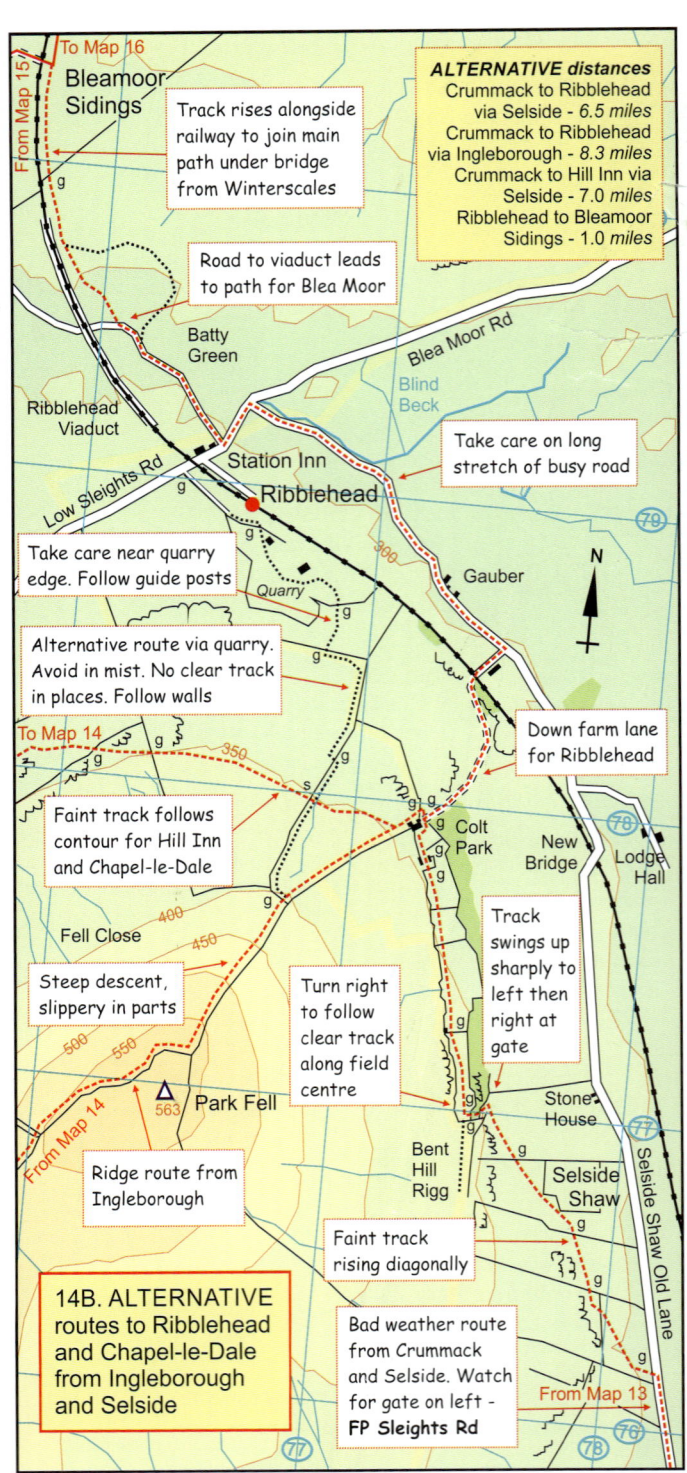

*Above:* Blea Moor signal box and Winterscales Beck at dusk.

*Above:* NW ridge above Rigg End, Whernside.   *Below:* Dent Main Street

## 4. DENTDALE

### *Chapel-le-Dale to Sedbergh (15.7 miles)*

The entire path from Chapel-le-Dale to Dent follows an ancient packhorse route, the Craven Way, which comes up from Ingleton. From Dent another old packhorse trail leads over Frostrow to Sedbergh.

A visit to St. Leonard's Church in the tiny hamlet of Chapel-le-Dale is a worthy pilgrimage, for here lie the remains of many of the navvies and their families who perished through accident and disease building the Settle-Carlisle railway.

At Bruntscar an option to climb Whernside - Yorkshire's highest peak - presents itself and may prove irresistible in fine weather. Otherwise it's on to Winterscales to pass beneath the awesome Ribblehead Viaduct, a man-made edifice which actually enhances the bleak natural beauty of the landscape.

The alternative route from Ribblehead joins here.

Ribblehead Viaduct is a quarter of a mile long with 24 arches. Every 6th one is called a King's Arch and is stronger so that if one arch collapsed it would take only a short section with it. The viaduct stands 104 feet above the surrounding moorland on piers sunk through 25 feet of peat and clay to the solid rock below. It was said that the viaduct was "built on wool", alluding to the fact that the Midland Railway's backers included wealthy Bradford wool merchants, but rumoured locally to mean the shafts were packed with bales of wool.

Passing the lonely signal box, the path leaves the railway which tunnels under Blea Moor, its continued route being marked by the ventilation shaft mounds that march across the rising fell. After a steep climb the walk around Whernside's northern flank is delightful and finally, at Wold's End, Dentdale opens out below in all its stunning beauty.

This is, in our opinion, the greenest and loveliest of the Yorkshire Dales. Ahead lies the village of Dent. Founded by Norse settlers, Dent was formally the major settlement in the region and until the 1930s there were over 20 shops along its Main Street.

Through Dent's narrow cobbled streets and past the towering 12$^{th}$ century church stands a large granite slab, monument to Adam Sedgwick (1785-1873), one of the founders of modern geology and Dent's most famous son. The area is also renowned for its hand knitting industry, an important supplement to farming incomes in the 18$^{th}$ century. The Heritage Centre details the history of the dale and is well worth a visit.

The Dales Way is joined for a short riverside walk before the climb over Frostrow to Sedbergh, where the lovely, steep-sided rolling hills of the Howgill Fells beckon.

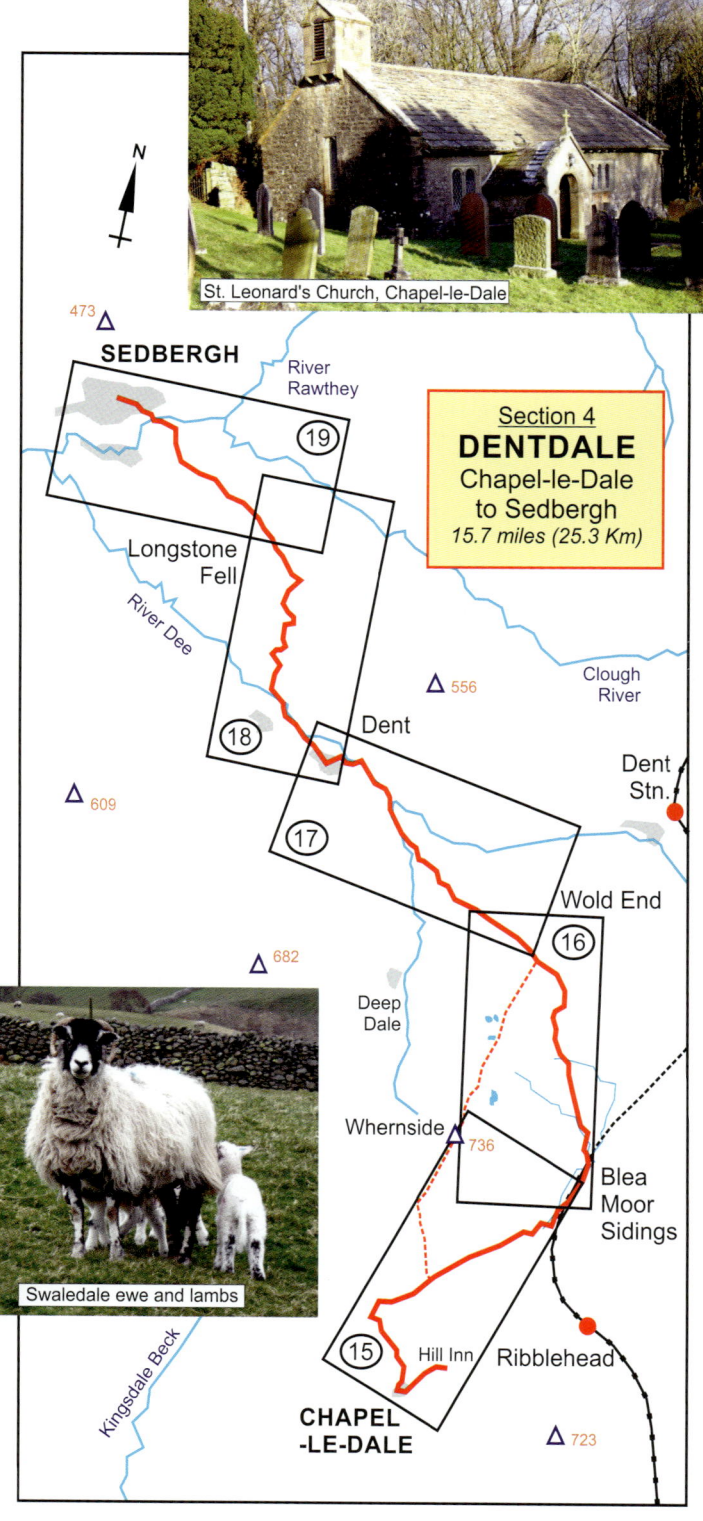

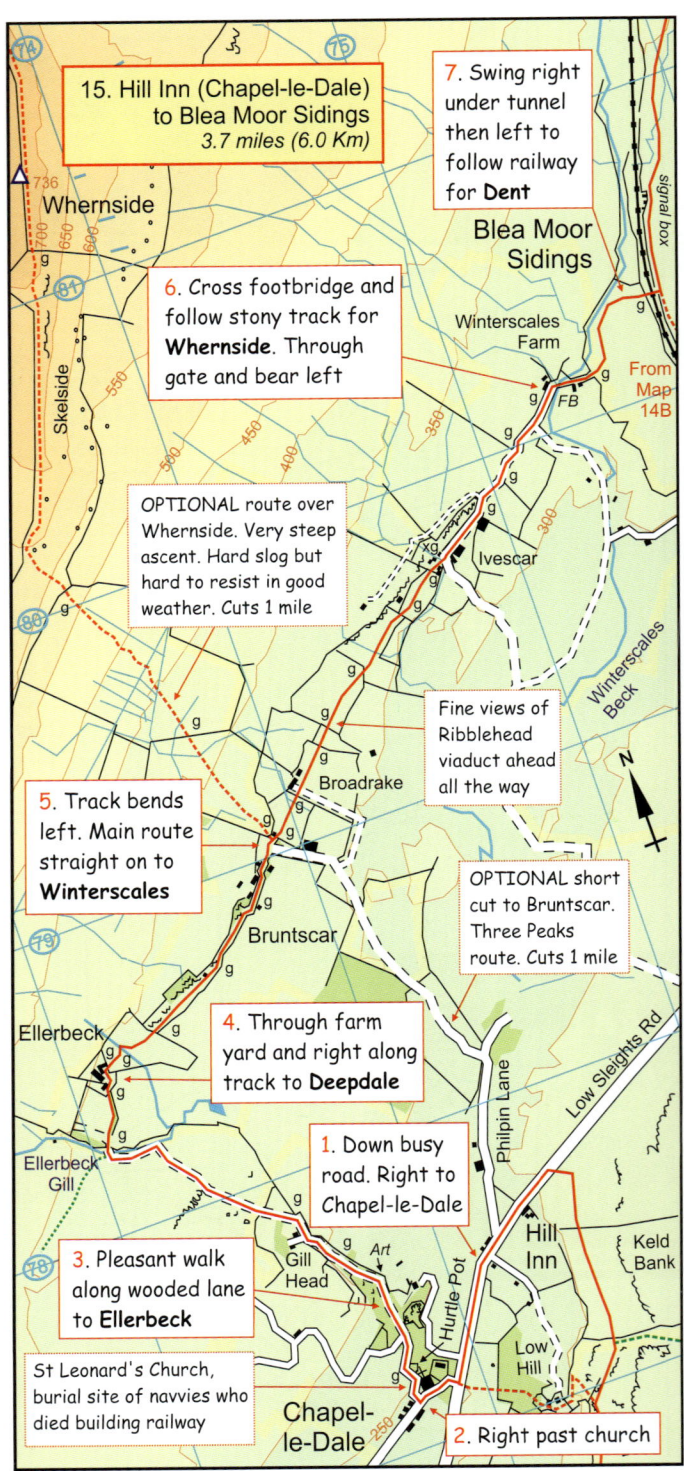

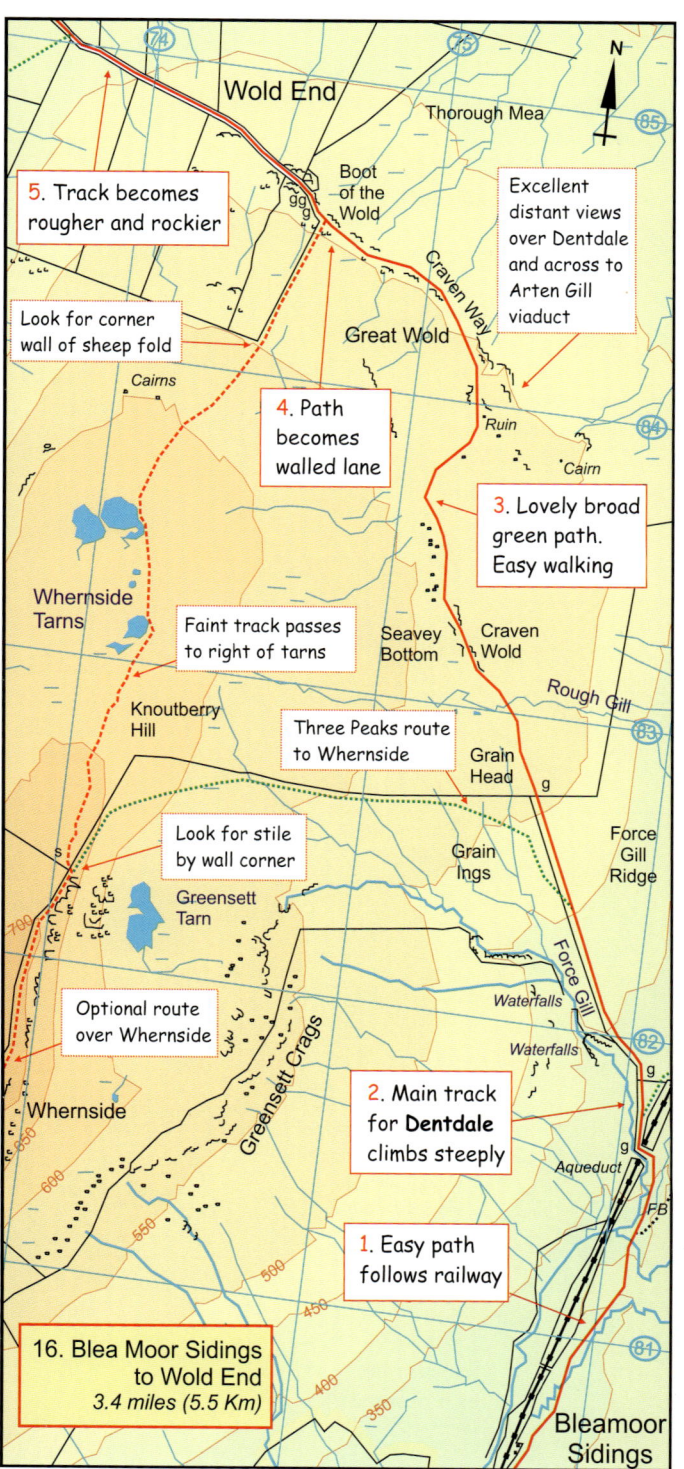

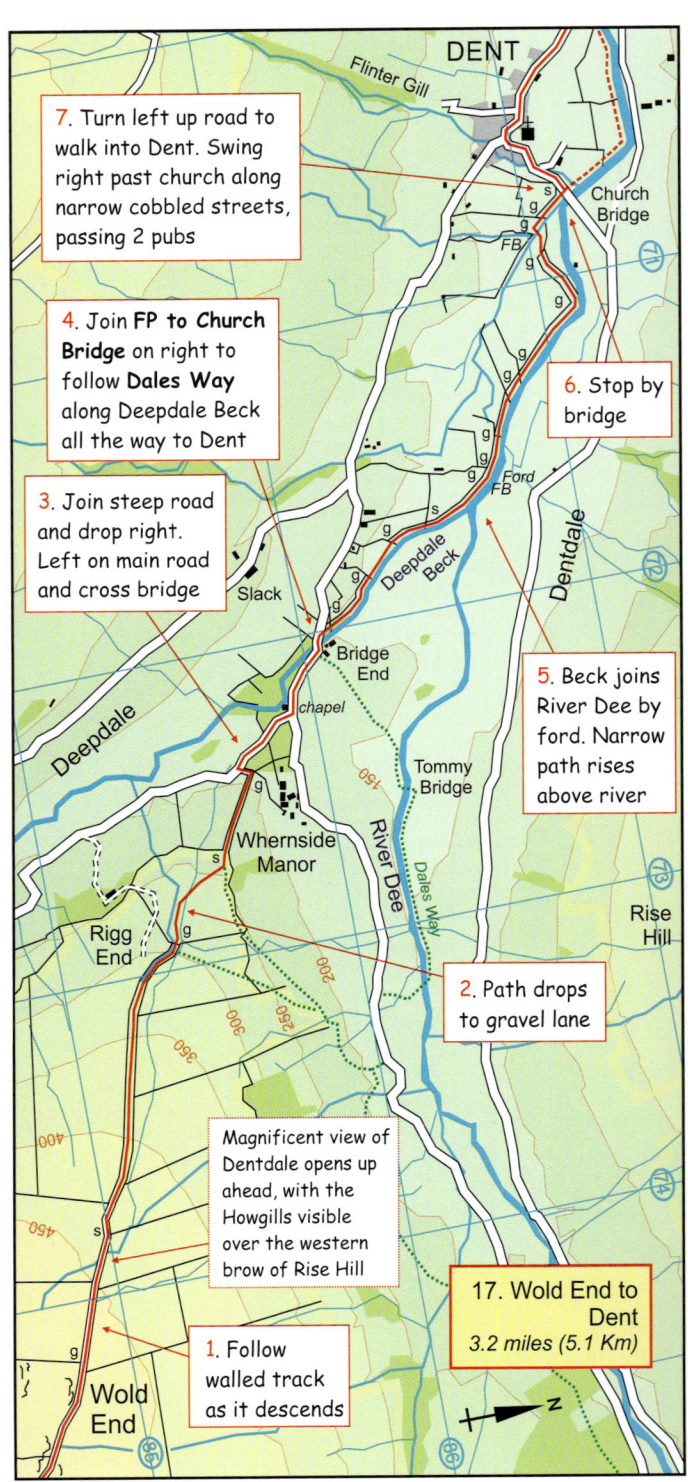

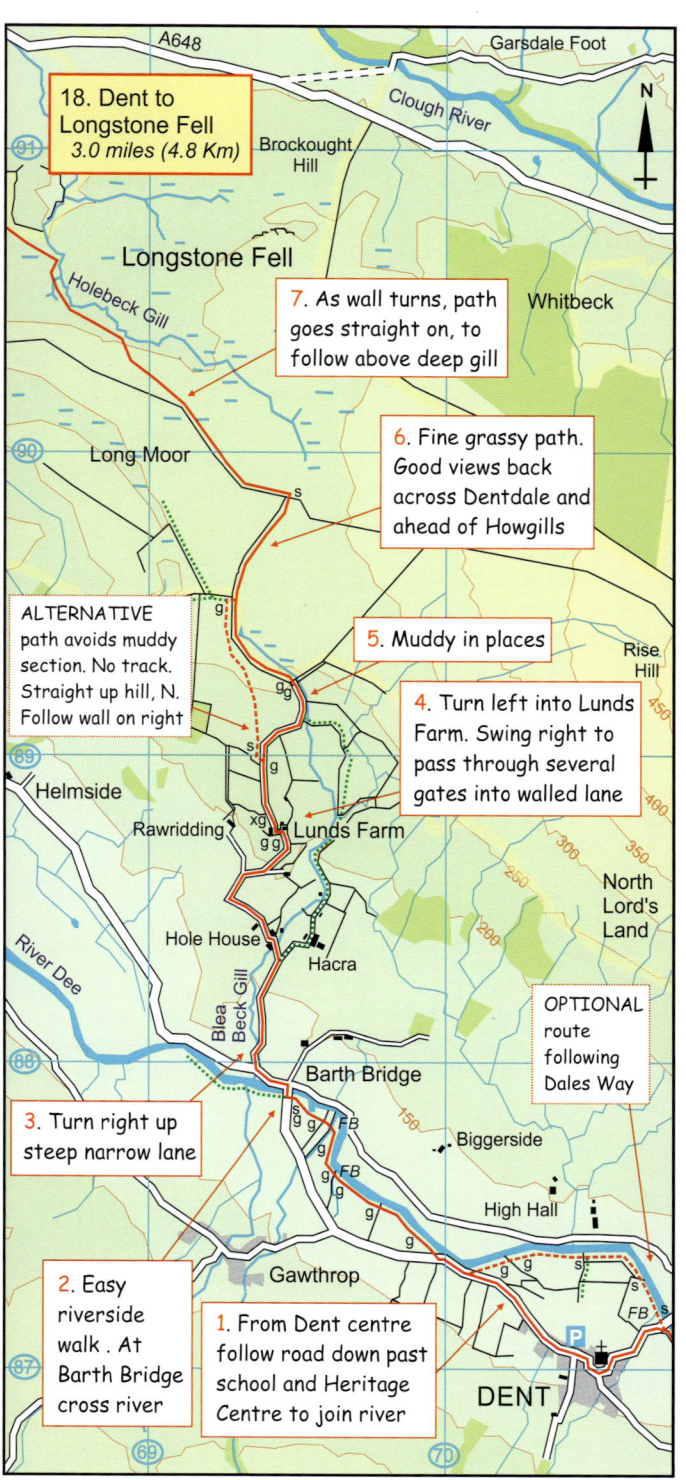

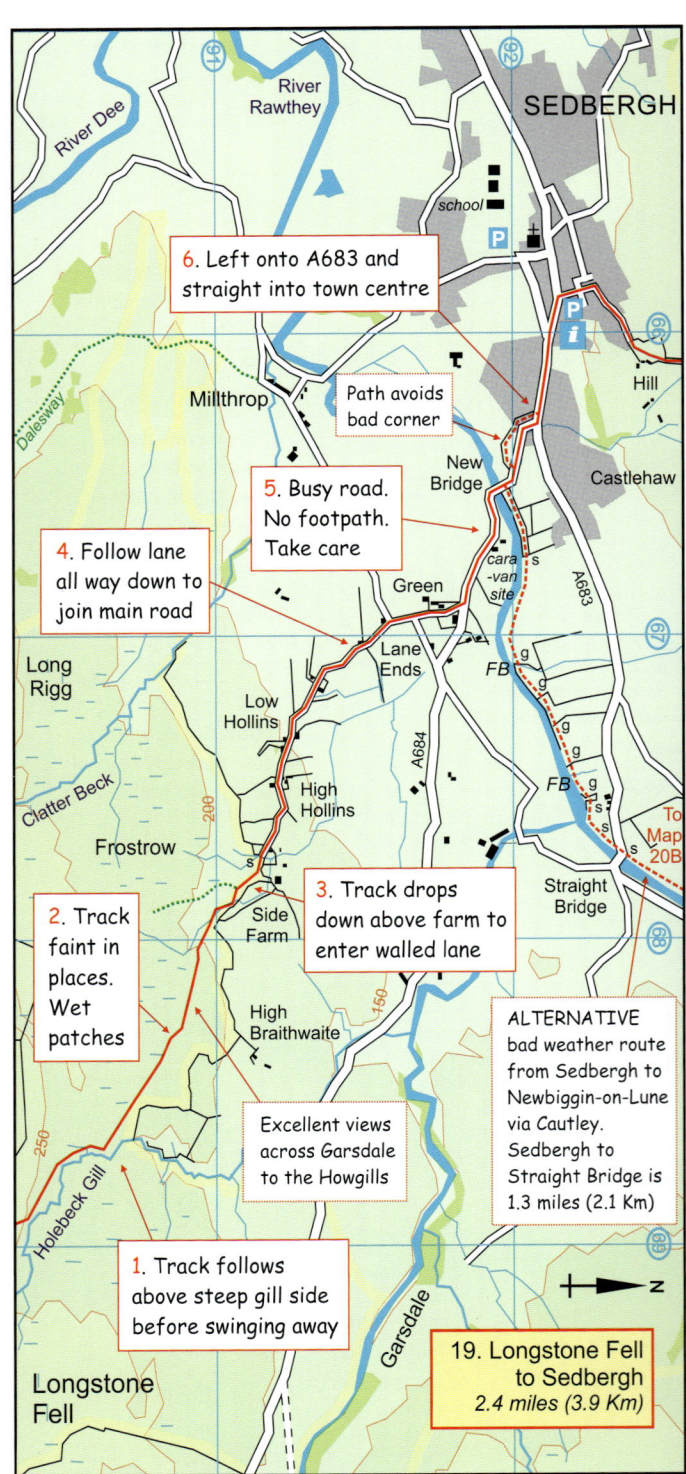

*Above:* Knott and Calders from Frostrow.

*Above:* Looking west from the ridge.  *Below:* Cautley Crags and the Rawthey.

# 5. HOWGILL FELLS

## *Sedbergh to Newbiggin-on-Lune (10.9 miles)*

The route now crosses the entire Howgill Fell range in a breathtaking six mile ridge walk. It is the shortest section, so there's time to linger and take in the distant views: the Three Peaks to the south-east; the adjoining Mallerstang-Garsdale range of Baugh, Swarth and Wild Boar Fells to the east; the magnificent Lakeland Fell skyline to the west; and the Orton Fells and Pennines that await to the north.

Time too to explore Sedbergh, England's official Book Town, with its cobbled yards and historic buildings. St Andrew's Church, dating from around 1130, is probably the oldest building in the town. George Fox, the founder of the Quakers, preached in the area many times, including under the yew tree in the churchyard. His most famous meeting was held outdoors on Firbank Fell where he addressed over 1,000 people from a rock known as Fox's Pulpit.

The Quaker tradition has long been influential in Sedbergh. The Quaker Meeting House at nearby Brigflatts was built in 1675 and is the oldest meeting house in the North of England. It retains many original oak furnishings and is still used today.

The Howgills are unique in character: steep sided, round topped, velvety folds in a compact group that separates the rough craggy mountains of Lakeland from the bleak peaty Pennine hills. Built on ancient, very hard Silurian slate and sandstone laid down in warm seas 400 million years ago and then uplifted, the Howgills are probably a far eastern extension of the Lakeland range. The rock is mostly unseen however, except at Cautley Crags, being covered by generally dry rough grass that makes the going easy.

The fells are open, with no walls to follow and no stiles to cross. Consequently care needs to be taken as the peaks and ridges are difficult to distinguish and in mist it is easy to get lost on the tops. With a little luck you'll catch sight of the semi-wild ponies roaming free over the open fells.

From the trig point at the Calf, the highest point on the Howgills, the route continues along the ridge above Bowderdale. A little careful navigation is required here, to avoid dropping too early into Langdale to the west. If mist comes in unexpectedly, the old drove route swinging right to drop into the long Bowderdale valley makes for a safe way down should it be needed. If the weather is too bad to start, then an interesting alternative route around the eastern flanks of the range adds less than a mile overall.

Newbiggin-on-Lune is a small village with plenty of accommodation but, alas, no pub or shop. If desperate, a further mile or so brings you to the lovely village of Ravenstonedale, which has both. But this, of course, adds a mile or so to the start of the last leg.

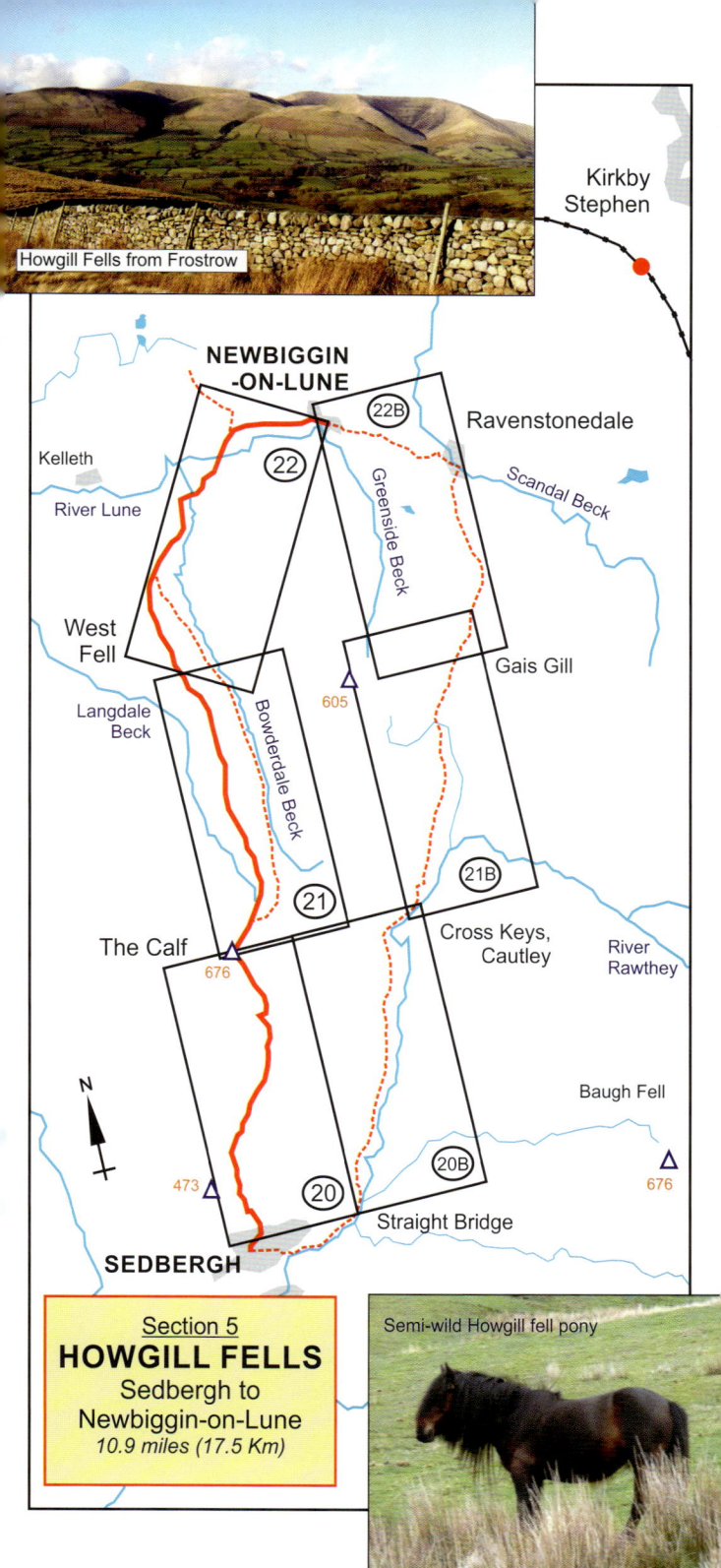

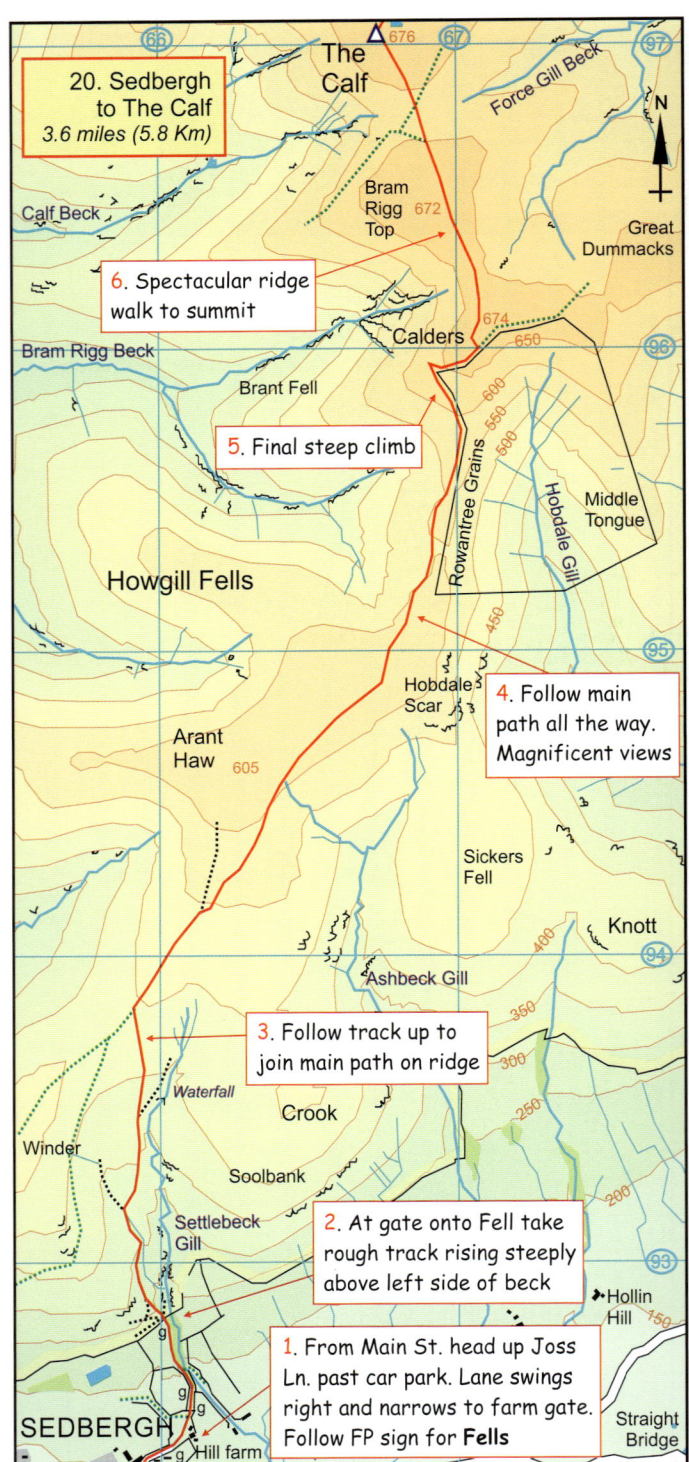

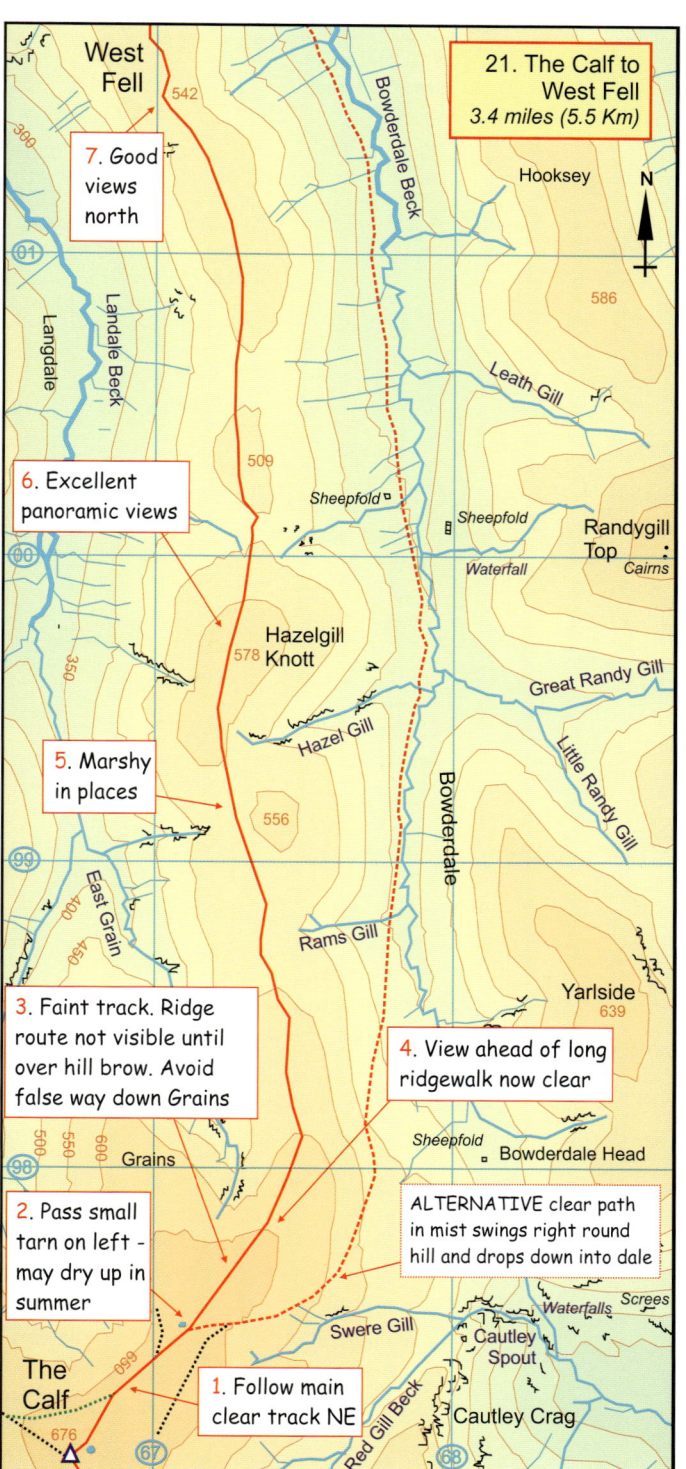

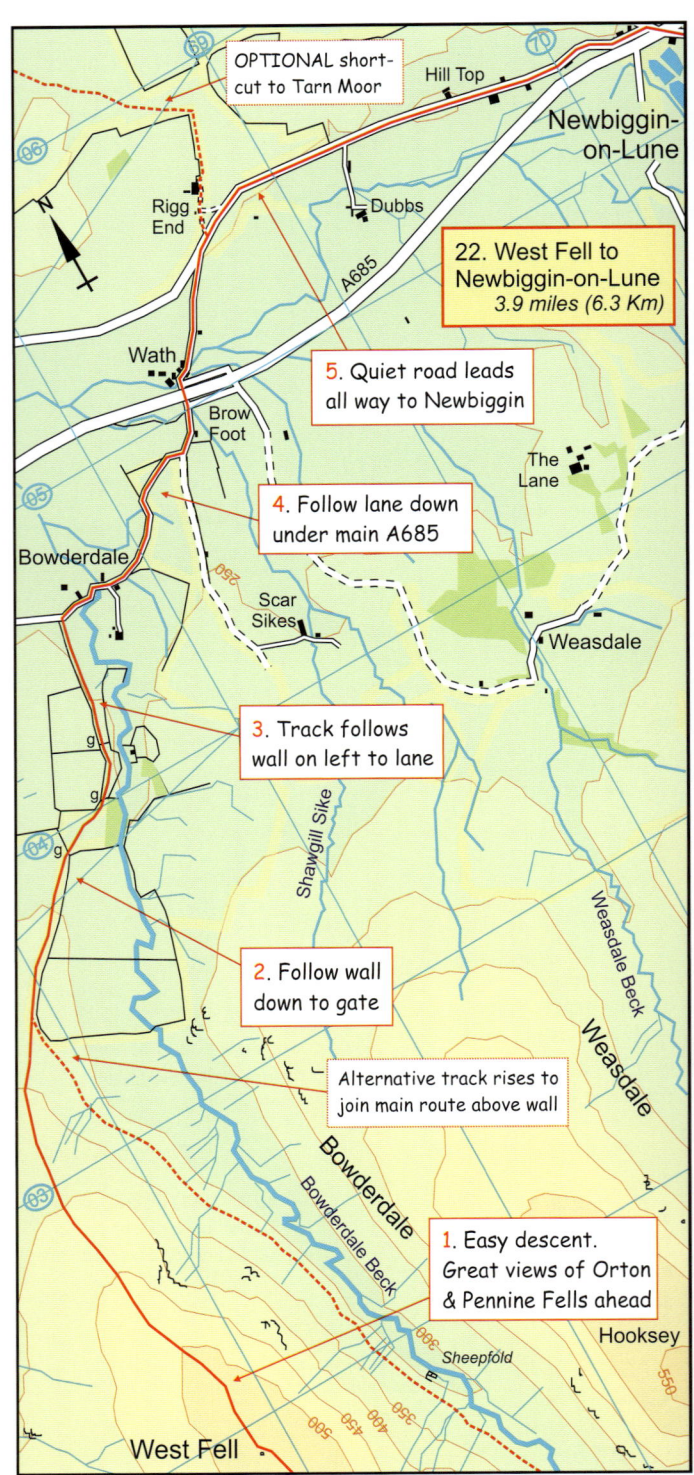

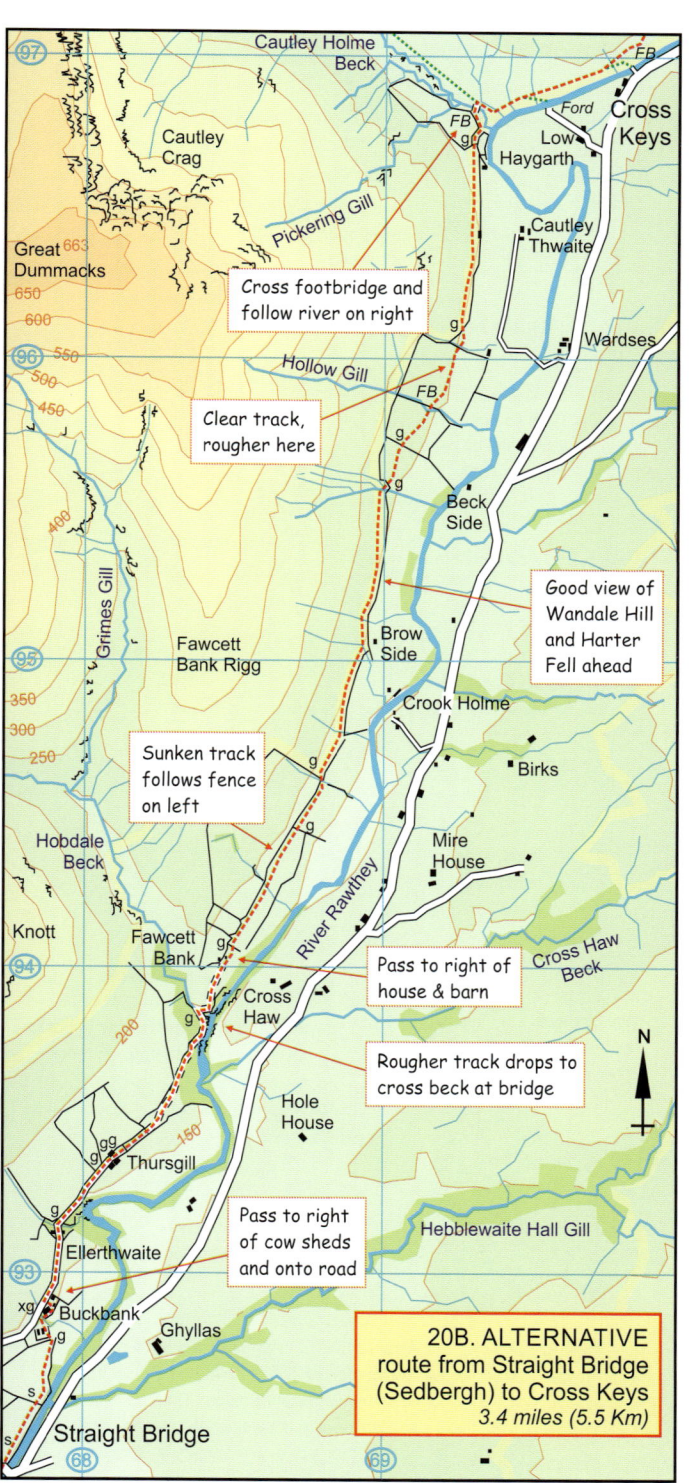

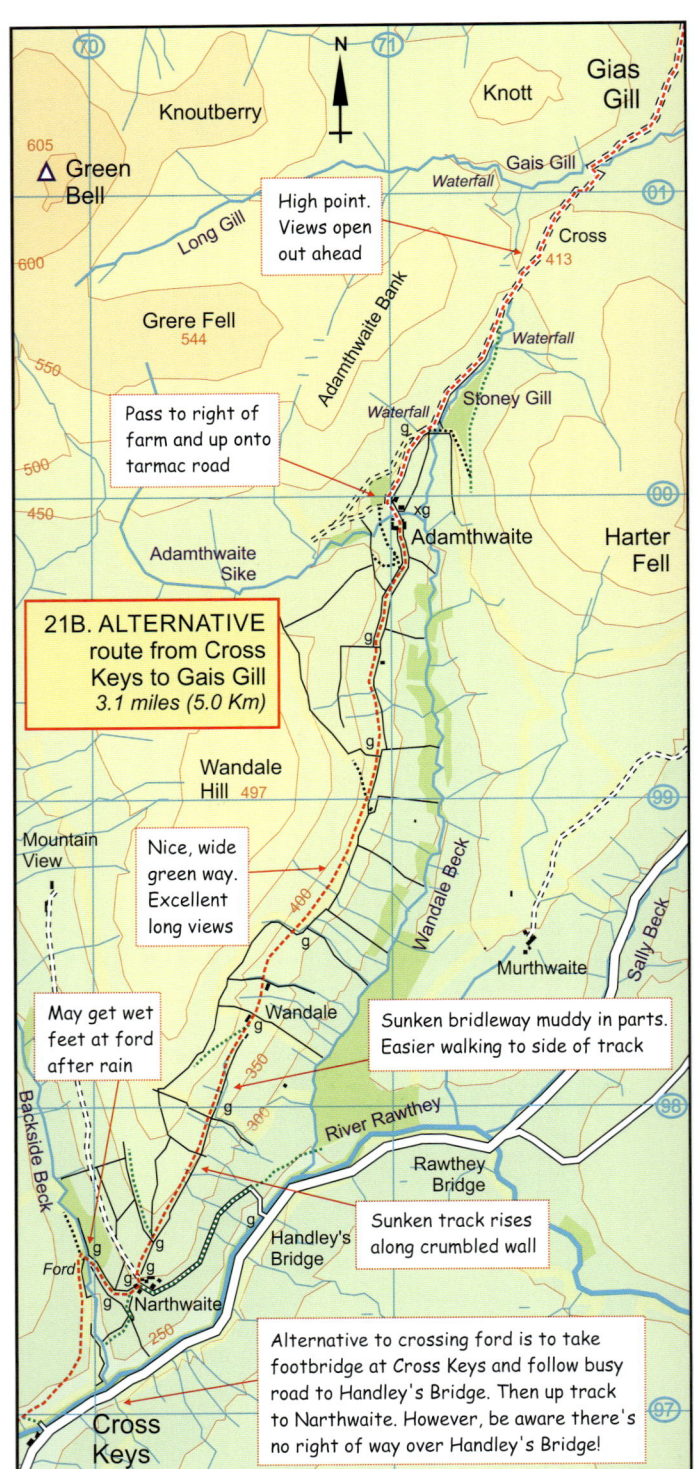

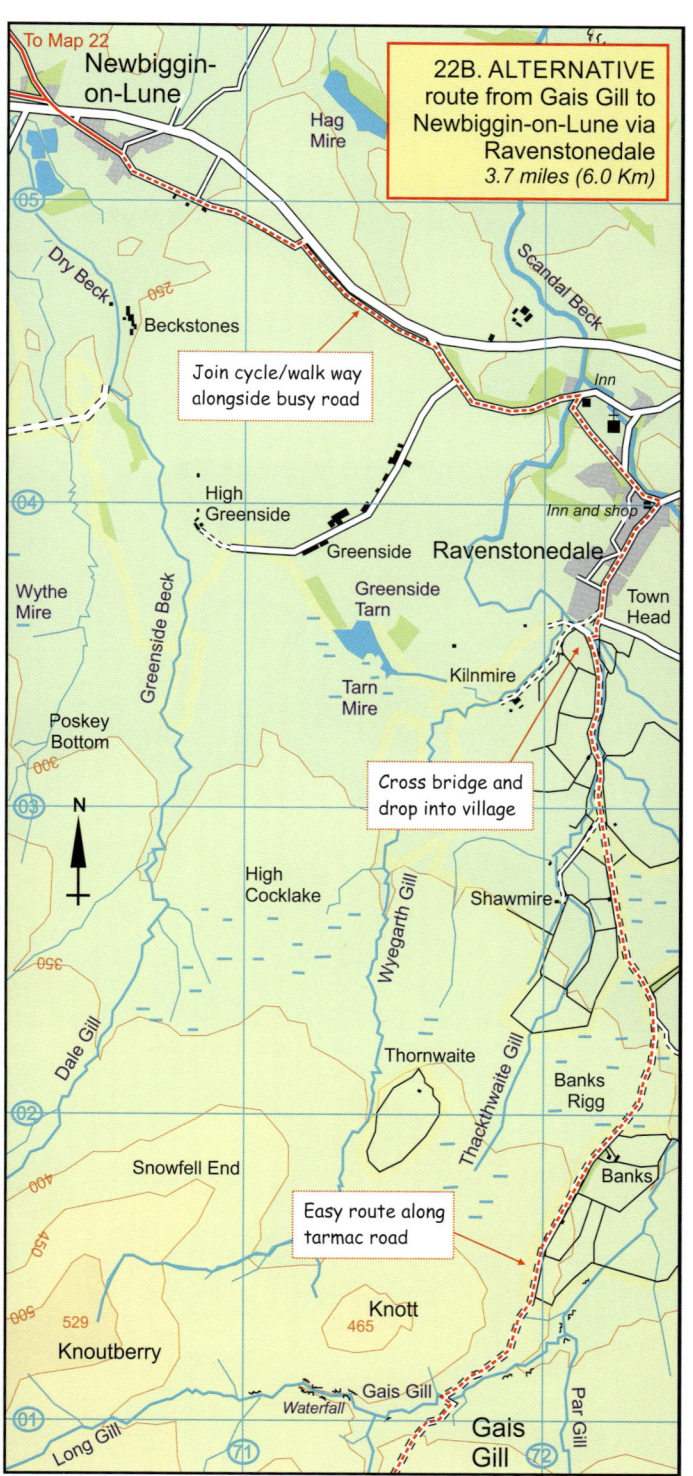

*Above:* Steam train crosses Ribblehead viaduct.

*Above:* Rutter Force and Mill.   *Below:* View from Appleby Bridge.

## THE PEOPLE WHO SHAPED THE DALES

Throughout prehistory people crossed the Yorkshire landscape along the fell and moor edges, avoiding the dark swampy valley bottoms. Here too they built their settlements.

The Roman occupation left little lasting impact on the Dales, save for a few roads and forts. The Romans struggled to subdue the local Brigantes and, when they left, life continued much as it had done before. In the 7th century Angles arrived from the south, and later the Vikings - the Danes and the Norse - settled and established farms and hamlets which survive to this day. Many place names (endings like -by, -thorpe, -thwaite) as well as words (dale, gill, beck, crag, fell and scar) are Scandinavian. They practised mixed farming, cultivating strip terraces and raising sheep.

Following the Norman invasion 1,000 years ago, William the Conqueror left the Pennines as "wasteland" to a handful of barons, who in turn gave generously to the Cistercian monks. The inhospitable terrain suited their desire for isolation. They built abbeys - Rievaulx, Kirkstall, Jervaulx and Fountains - and established huge monastic estates across the Dales on which to raise sheep on an industrial scale. Fountains alone had over 1 million acres, including much of Malhamdale and Ribblesdale.

*"Packhorses"*
*from W.H.Payne's "Microcosm" 1803*

Drove roads and packhorse trails developed linking villages, farms, market towns and abbeys. Sticking still largely to the high country, they made their way from place to place as directly as the terrain would allow.

A period of relative prosperity for Dales folk followed the dissolution of the monasteries in 1536 and most of the wooden houses were rebuilt with stone. Packhorse trains remained the foremost form of transport up until the 19th century, when the growth of Turnpike (toll) roads, along with the railways and canals, which generally followed the lower valley routes with easier gradients, brought the era of the packhorse to an end.

The last major feature of the modern Dales landscape appeared following the Enclosures Acts in the 19th century, when thousands of miles of dry stone walls parcelled the land.

# 6. EDEN VALLEY

## *Newbiggin-on-Lune to Appleby  (12.7 miles)*

The final section of the walk has a relaxed, winding down feel to it. It begins with a short hike over Ravenstonedale Moor to reach the isolated splendour of Sunbiggin Tarn, an important place for migrating and resident birds and a Site of Special Scientific Interest. The easy moorland walking suggests that limestone country is now left far behind.

Then a surprise as the climb beside the humble peak of Great Kinmond reveals a vast expanse of spectacular limestone pavements. This is Great Asby Scar, part of the Orton Fell range that runs from Lakeland to the Pennines along the side of the River Lune and sports the finest limestone pavements in the UK outside the Ingleborough area. Here also prehistoric humans have left their mark: Mesolithic flints and stones, Bronze Age stone circles and an Iron Age settlement atop the limestone escarpment at Castle Fold nearby.

The views from the top are stunning as the Eden Valley opens out ahead backed by the towering northern Pennine skyline, with the Lakeland Fells now close by to the west and the Howgills behind.

The Pennine view accompanies the steady descent to Great Asby and beyond, where the last leg of the walk begins, following a lovely beckside ramble to the picturesque Rutter Mill and its delightful waterfall.

This lush green farmland is dairy country and unless you're walking in winter or early spring you're bound to run into grazing cattle. If this troubles you, there are many alternative routes nearby along fairly quiet country lanes.

The route continues alongside Hoff Beck, through Hoff itself and on to the ancient crossing at Bandley Bridge, before a final short climb brings the castle at Appleby and the final destination into view.

Appleby is an attractive market town with an old-fashioned charm. Boroughgate, the broad main street, has been described as the finest in England. The walking is over, but the journey has yet to reach its climax with the return to Saltaire on the Settle-Carlisle line: England's most beautiful railway.

The line runs from Carlisle through to Leeds, but undoubtedly the most spectacular section is the one from Appleby to Settle. The long climb to the summit at Ais Gill between Mallerstang on the left and Wild Boar Fell on the right is awesome. From Dent station, the highest in the land, you are treated to a succession of highlights from the walk: through Blea Moor tunnel, across Ribblehead Viaduct and past the mighty Ingleborough. Beyond Settle the landscape is gentler but no less beautiful. Finally, the train passes the golden mill at Saltaire and your journey is over.

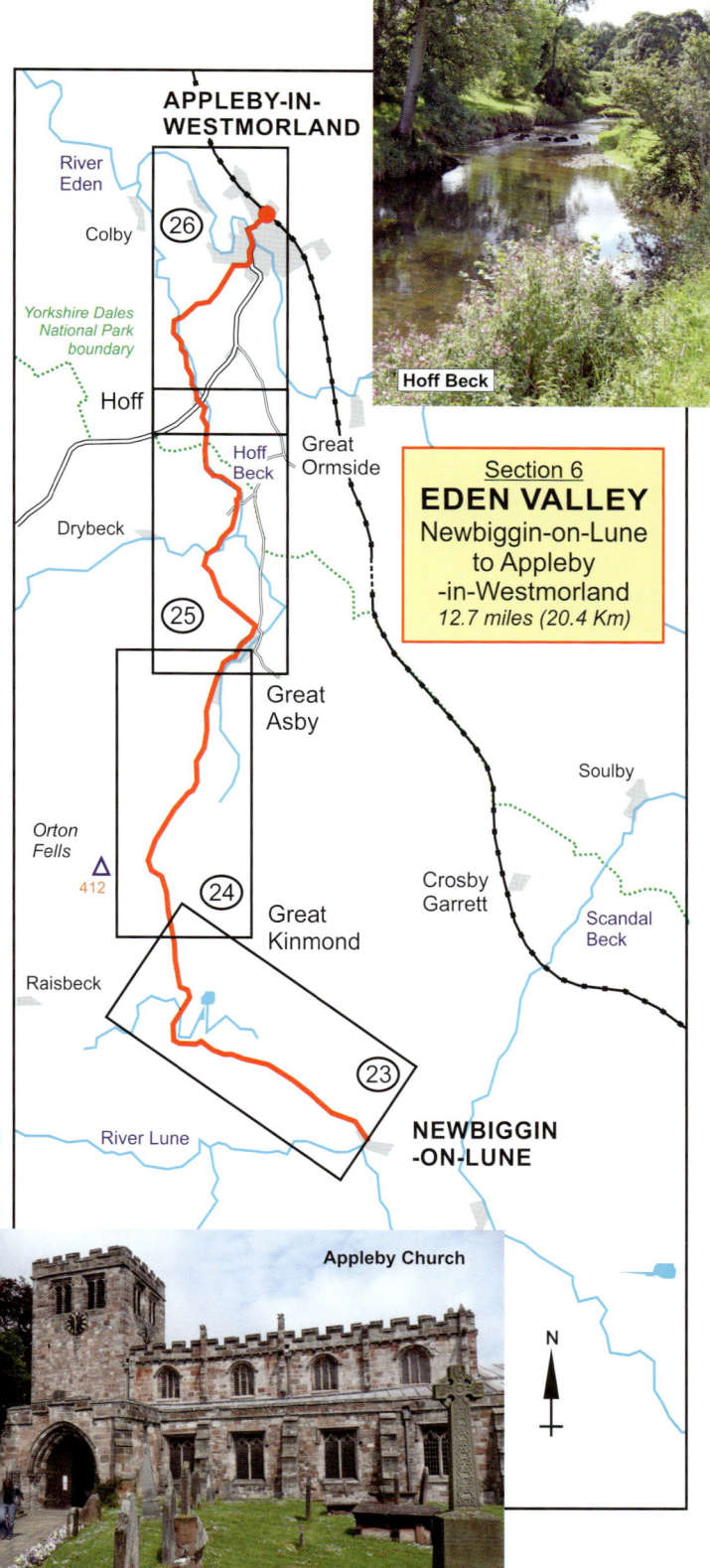

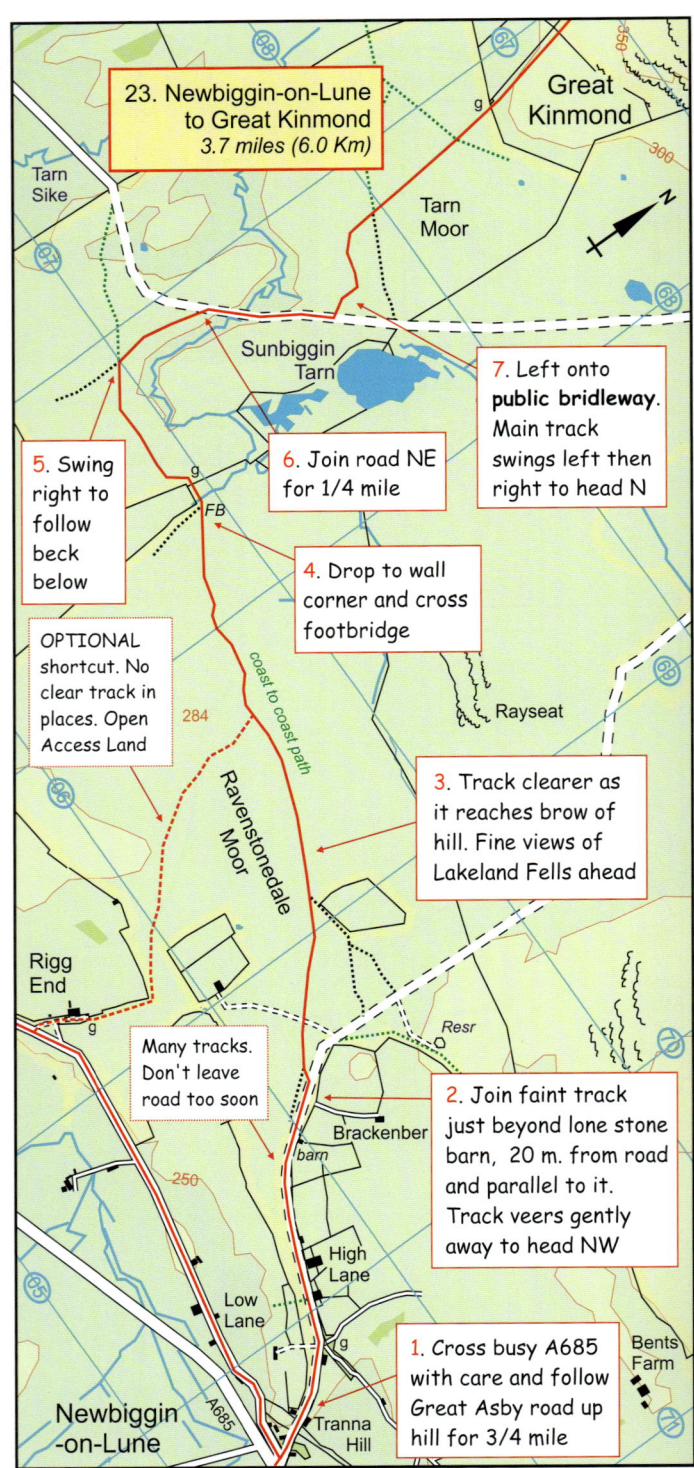

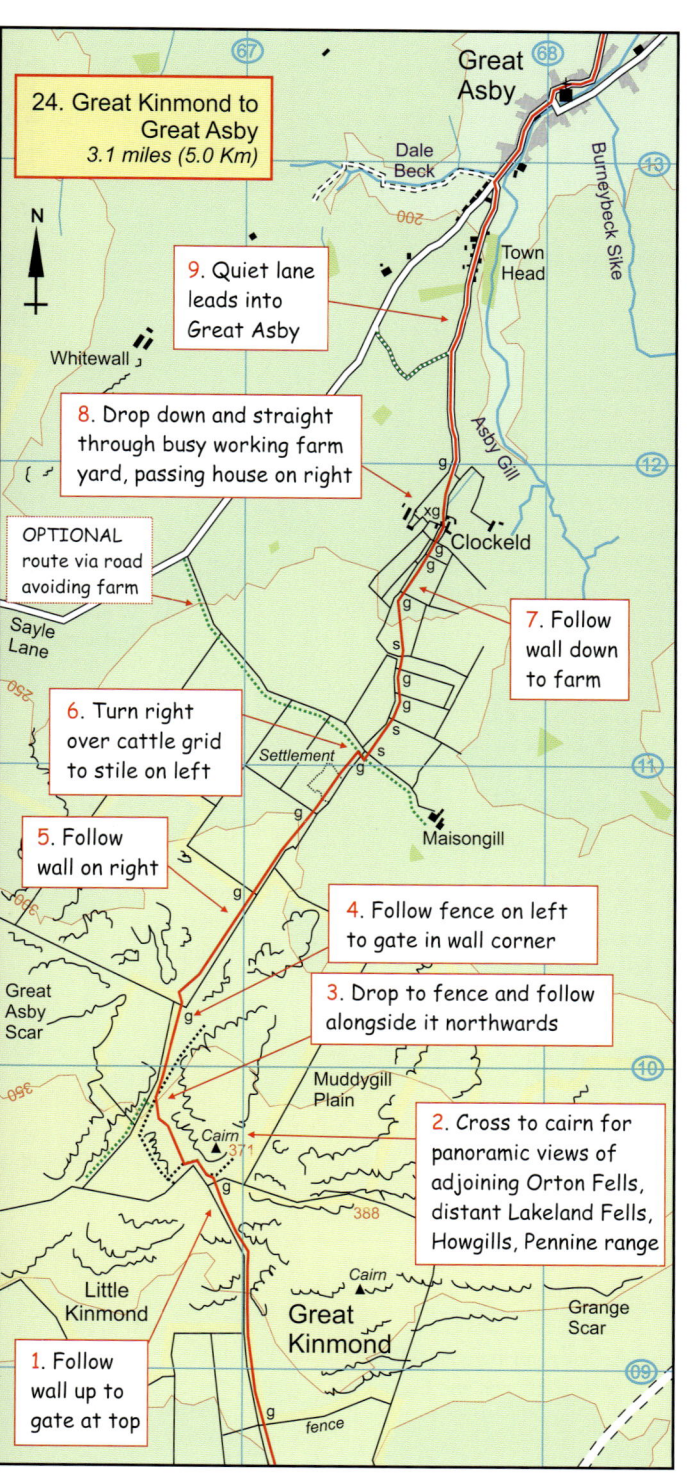

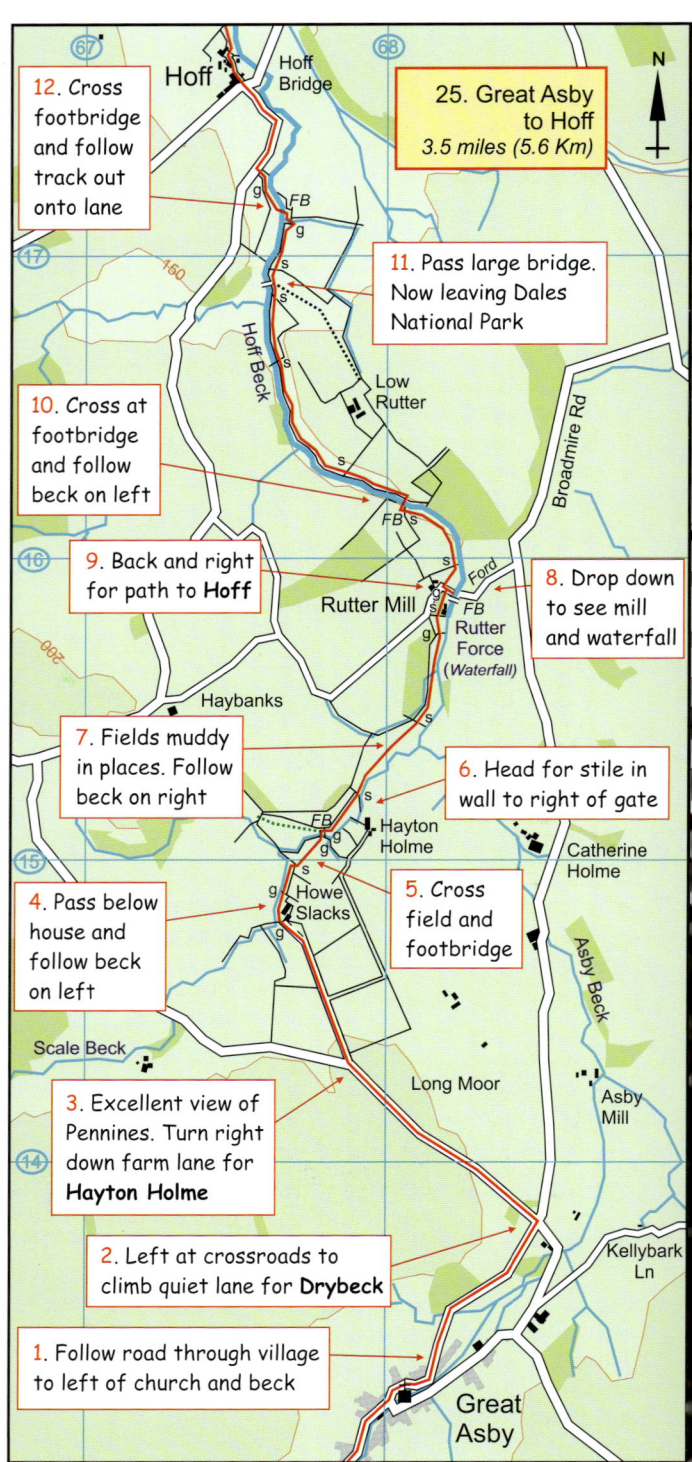